CW01656531

ƆN

THE DOG OWNERS SELF-ISOLATION SURVIVAL GUIDE

Discover how to quickly and easily exercise, entertain, and emotionally connect with your dog, from the seclusion of your sitting room.

Published by
www.elitepublishingacademy.com

First Edition published 2020

Printed and bound in Great Britain by
www.elitepublishingacademy.com

A catalogue record for this book
is available from The British Library

ISBN 978-1-912713-64-6

Contents

Foreword

Why write a book about self-isolating with a dog?

For those reading this sometime way in the future, it might indeed seem a little odd to write a book about how to exercise your dog while you are locked away in your home.

But, for where the world is at the time of me writing this, in late March 2020, locked in the grip of the Coronavirus outbreak which looks like being the scariest and widespread medical emergency in the last 100 years, it feels like the right thing to do.

I'm Dom Hodgson, a dog lover, a dog owner, a dog trainer, and a writer of dog training books.

Trainers *teach* and writers *write*, so writing this book feels like the best way for me to be of service to the dog lovers in my world who need help, and the wider canine community.

This book will help pet dog owners who are self-isolating, pet professionals who are looking for ways to help their distressed clients, and of course, the dogs themselves, who are going to have to deal with their changes to their daily routine.

In short, this book will help you exercise, entertain and emotionally connect with your dog (or dogs) during a self-isolation period.

These are truly terrifying times, but as a dog owner, you have a leg up (or four legs up) on those who are self-isolating alone.

At a time when many people are afraid and alone, without human or animal company, you actually have your best friend with you, and that should be a hugely comforting thought.

On the other hand, self-isolating on your own means you only have yourself to look after.

As a dog owner, who maybe owns more than one dog, you have to find a way to give your dog everything he needs to be a happy and contented pet. This won't be easy when there are restrictions of movement in place, or maybe temporarily impossible if a lock-down situation comes into effect.

This book will give you a road-map that guides you through a self-isolation period, and gives you the tools to ensure your dog is physically and mentally well exercised and stimulated, which will prevent any bored and destructive behaviours developing while you are both cooped up indoors. And it will also help keep your dog closer to you when you are walking him outdoors, so you can easily give him the opportunity to exercise like a dog, whilst allowing you to comply with any social-distancing restrictions that are in place.

And, most importantly of all, it will enable you to have fun with your dog, whose company will be sorely needed by you during these stressful times. As you'll see later, self-isolation could actually be the making of a new, better, more connected relationship between you and your dog.

Without further ado, let's dive in!

Introduction

If you are a dog owner living through the current Corona-virus outbreak, then you'll no doubt be experiencing the same anxious, dark reality that your non-dog owning friends are going through.

And when your world is plunged into uncertainty, and the constant news about the pandemic can feel relentless, it won't be long before the stress and worry start to take its toll on your mental health.

Unfortunately, this book is not a vaccine against Covid-19, but it will certainly act as an 'antidote' to loneliness and help you and your dog cope with self-isolation and social distancing.

People are worried right now.

There are concerns for jobs, businesses, family members and our future way of life.

There are lots of uncertainties and unknowns about the future.

One thing we know for certain is our dogs currently play a huge roll in our lives, and that won't change during, or after the crises.

And as dog owners, we have a responsibility to keep providing everything our dogs need to remain healthy and happy.

This book will help you do that.

In fact, it has the potential to do much more.

Our dogs can provide a useful distraction in times of distress.

I personally know many people who feel they have been 'saved' by their dogs, specifically from the comfort and support they've received from their caring canine companions.

Dogs have the ability to take our mind off bad news, protect us in times of danger and even pull us out of depression.

And as a dog owner, I think you have the perfect companion to help you through all the tough times you may go through in your life. And no, I don't mean your partner or children, I'm referring to the four-legged furball who is lying in the corner of your room, snoring softly.

How your dog can help you deal with a crisis

During the early stages of the Coronavirus pandemic, the WHO (World Health Organisation) published some advice on mental health and dealing with stress during the outbreak.

Some of their recommendations include;

- Avoid watching, reading or listening to news that could cause you to feel anxious or distressed.
- Seek information to take practical steps to prepare plans and protect yourself and your loved ones.
- Seek information at specific times during the day once or twice. The sudden and near-constant stream of

news reports about an outbreak can cause anyone to feel worried.

This book will give you the practical plan of action you need to give your dog all the mental and physical exercise he needs which will, in turn, help protect you both.

You need structure when self-isolating with your dog.

It has long been known that dogs give owners, particularly elderly owners, a real sense of purpose, and help them create a routine that brings structure to their day.

My aim is that the easy to follow training in this book will also provide some much-needed structure to your day when self-isolating.

Your dog still needs walking, attention, exercise, interaction, feeding and an opportunity to feel 'like a dog'.

All of the activities in this book are things you can do at home, whether you live in a house with a garden or yard, a flat or apartment with no immediate outside access, and even a caravan.

And, self-isolation can also be a tremendous opportunity for you and your dog to spend some much-needed quality time together. As a full-time business owner, I know how work, kids and life in general can often get in the way of you enjoying your dog.

Most of us bring a dog into our lives so we can do new things and enjoy more time together in the great outdoors. Unfortunately, the blissful long walk with the dog tends to be something we only get to enjoy on weekends, and the rest of the week is about finding a quick ten-minutes in our busy schedule to take him for a toilet break.

Well, if you are stuck at home self-isolating, you now have the time to build a better relationship with your dog, as well as catch up on all your Netflix series, and decorate your kitchen…

And, self-isolation can also present a great opportunity for you to start fixing some of your dog's behavioural problems.

How to use self-isolation to re-connect with your dog

At the heart of many dog behaviour problems lies a lack of connection to the owner.

By lack of connection, I don't mean you don't love your dog, of course you do. But, how much does your dog love you?

Well, he might enjoy getting cuddles on the couch while you are chilling out watching Netflix together, but how much attention does he pay you outside at the park, beach or woods, when there are other distractions around?

Does he love you more than he loves chasing squirrels, rolling in dead animals, running off to play with other dogs, or following his nose to find leftover pizza under the park bench?

See, that's the true measure of how much your dog loves you.

Does he prefer to be with you *even when* there are, what he perceives to be, more fun options around?

If your dog would rather wander off and play hooky than be with you, then you need to show him/teach him/convince him, how much fun you really are.

Don't worry though, by the end of this book your dog will look at you like you are his superhero.

How self-isolation can help you get to know your dog

An extended period of time at home self-isolating is actually the perfect opportunity for you to take your dog away from the distractions he finds hard to ignore, and teach him that you are the most fun person in the (and especially his) world.

So, I'm going to start in Chapter one by helping you rebuild, re-kindle, re-energise your relationship with your dog with an easy and fun 'dog audit' which you can do in your living room.

Let's get cracking!

Chapter One

Finding the Kryptonite

'Control the toy, control the dog'
John Rogerson

I remember the first time I saw anyone approach training a dog by actually asking the dog what he liked. I was attending a seven-day dog behaviour course with John Rogerson, who is widely regarded as the forefather of modern dog training. The course involved a lot of listening but also lots of opportunities to get hands-on with a dog too. We were housed in a learning centre that was part of the Darlington Dogs Trust rehoming centre, and so we had access to some of the dogs that were there awaiting a new home.

The first dog was brought in, and John proceeded to ask the dog a series of questions, but not in 'Parkinson' style. He offered the dog a series of tests, and he was quickly able to gather a lot of information about the dog. For example, he fed the dog a biscuit, and because the dog took the biscuit very gently, you could reasonably assume that the dog had been fed by humans and maybe even children. He showed him another dog across the room, and when he whined to get to him, it appeared fairly obvious that the dog had maybe lived with another dog or certainly had access to other dogs. This went on for some time until we were able to build a fairly accurate picture of what type of things this particular dog had learned to do in his life. For more information on exactly how John does this, you should check out his excellent book, *The Dog Vinci Code.*

I subsequently learned this is how a lot of trainers and behaviourists assess a dog, the good ones anyway. My friend and colleague David Davies, also a dog trainer, sends a questionnaire to the dog owners, and from the answers, he will have a pretty good idea of why they may be having a certain kind of problem with their dog.

There are many tests you can give a dog, but I have tried to narrow it down to the bare minimum you should do to help you solve the problems you are having with your own dog.

We have been gradually gathering some very basic information about your dog, but now it's time to deep dive into this and find the Kryptonite. These tests are easy, and they are fun, and they are exactly what I drove straight home and did with my own dogs as soon as the course ended that day.

I have split the audit up into five sections, but you can add more categories if you wish.

The information we are looking to gather straightaway is as follows:

- Your dog's five favourite foods – out of everything he ever eats.
- Your dog's five favourite toys – or things he likes playing with. This should include stuff you don't like him playing with, but it's still safe to use, e.g. hairbrushes and slippers.
- Your dog's five favourite touch points – where he loves being stroked, touched, or tickled.
- Your dog's five favourite locations – where are the places he goes that get him really excited? Rank them in order.

- Your dog's five favourite people – should be pretty obvious, but we are going to find out and again rank them in order.

There are two reasons why completing the dog audit will act as a successful kick-starter for all the training that follows.

The first is the information you are going to gather. Knowing what makes your dog's tail wag is very powerful information that we are going to leverage to get him interested in us. Once you have completed this, you will know what and who he likes and loves, but also where he is most distracted and shows his bad behaviour.

You can then avoid these places, which will make the playing and the training much easier. Later in the book, I have some strategies to make your actual walks less stressful when your self-isolation period is over.

The second reason is the process you go through to find that information requires you to get on the floor and interact with your dog. This is the part many people are afraid of and think, 'What if my… doesn't like me?' My advice is JFDI (just *flipping do it – or insert appropriate swear word *here).

Look, you now know why your dog does the bad things he currently does, and you know he can't unlearn them, so it's your job to teach him something new instead. I promise you this process will be fun, so let's do it. I say again: take your time and enjoy the process.

How do we find out what your dog likes? Quite simply, we ask him. We don't actually say, 'Oi Fido, what do you prefer, gravy bones or hot dogs?' Well, unless you are a dog whisperer and magically know through your Jedi mind tricks what he likes. For the rest of us mere mortals who have to use actual teachable training methods, we are going to ask our dogs another way.

We do this through trial and error and by seeing what he likes. We basically put something in front of him and observe how he reacts to it. Then we see if we can get him more interested in it by playing with it, and once he is wagging his tail, we get something else out and see which one he prefers.

That's a very brief overview, of course, and I am going to show you in much greater detail now how to go through the dog audit step by step.

Setting the scene

Before we begin, I want you to clear the room of any distractions. Remove any KONGS and toys and put any chews away. Then turn the TV off, put some music on that makes you feel happy (keep it fairly low volume though because you want your dog to be able to hear you talk). You should even lower the blinds or close the curtains if you feel a bit self-conscious about anyone peeping in and seeing you play the canine version of The Generation Game…

Then we can begin.

We are going to start with toys and touch and leave food till last. Why? Because food is obvious, and most dogs are interested in food, so please challenge yourself a bit and go with toys first.

I love playing with toys with my dogs. By far, the biggest revelation for me since I started my training and adventure business is just how much dogs love playing with toys with humans. You can get quite physical with a dog playing tuggy, and it's much easier to wear a dog out playing a retrieve game than it is walking or running with them. And remember dogs love a *challenge.* Dogs are strong, and they have powerful jaws they enjoy using. Dogs aren't allowed to put their teeth on human skin or our furniture, so it's good if you can provide a challenge that actually allows your dog to use his teeth in a controlled way.

But don't stress if you think your dog doesn't like toys as we are going to use food in a minute. Just have a go with toys anyway; you may surprise yourself.

Start by getting out what you think your dog's most desirable and pleasurable things are. Remember, this may not be a traditional dog toy; we are just looking for the thing or things that he loves holding. We can get him to interact with hairbrushes, socks, slippers, plastic bottles, towels, or anything that's safe and usable.

Put your five or six things on a table so your dog can't get the ones you aren't using, and get on the floor and PLAY.

Whoa there, Dom, did you say 'play'? What do you mean 'play'?

I mean play. OK, think of it more as interacting if playing is too much for your cold heart to handle at the moment. I'm just kidding… a little. Seriously, you need to P-L-A-Y. Why do you think we are doing this in the safety of our own homes with the curtains drawn so no one can see us making a fool of ourselves?

If we are going to re-build the relationship you have with your dog (and we definitely ARE going to do that), then we need to know what makes your four-legged friend tick. And we start by finding out exactly what he likes.

What makes your dog tick?

Try and remember what it felt like to play when you were five years old. Yes, it was a long time ago, wasn't it, but life was good, and you had next to nothing to worry about except which biscuit to eat, TV programme to watch, or game to play.

Carefree time pretending to be Spider-Man or Wonder Woman and rolling around building forts and playing armies or doctors and nurses. This is what I'm after here, and it's what your dog is after too. It bears repeating, but your dog wants some fun in his life. He probably already has fun, but it just doesn't involve you. Well, you are going to show this dog just how bloody fun you can be!

Toys

Toy exercise:

Get on the floor with a toy (or something he loves), and get his attention with it. By get his attention, I don't mean shove it in his face and say 'LOOK HERE, I HAVE FUN, PLAY NOW.' No, we are going to be a bit subtler than that.

We know that dogs almost always want stuff other people have, so if your dog isn't immediately interested in you, then you can tease your dog just a little. So in a nice cheery voice, you can say something like 'Oooh what's this I've got? Isn't this the most interesting and best slipper ever?' (Or whatever the thing is he likes). Then try and tempt your dog over to you with it. If you read and understood the previous part of this chapter, you will hopefully be using something you know your dog likes, so it shouldn't be too hard to get him to take some notice of you. You have something he wants after all.

Don't get disheartened if he doesn't jump up straight away; you will have to put in a bit of effort and encourage him. Try and get a bit of interaction going with the toy, but don't be tempted to just give it to him. The idea is you are teaching him to like you and like doing stuff with you because you have stuff he likes. Eventually, it won't matter what toy you use, but for now, use his favourite things and make things easy for yourself.

So now you have his attention, you can show him the 'Kryptonite'. Let him have a sniff of it, talk to him, and make him feel special.

Next, put that Kryptonite away, get one of the other items, and repeat the same thing. If you are on a roll with your dog, then, by all means, have more of a play with him, but keep switching between items.

You aren't actually playing with your dog at the moment. All you are looking for is your dog taking an interest in you and showing a desire to have the thing you have. If it's any consolation, your dog may feel a bit awkward too and may not know what to think of this new you. He may be thinking something like, 'Well, this is a new one, isn't it? She's never done this before' or, 'What can she be after?... 'Hmm, hang on though; she has that hairbrush I really like, so I better go and check it out. You never know, she might give it to me, and that would make me very happy indeed.' (And make sure you do a silly dog voice when you read that part too!)

So it's going to take a bit of time but stick with it. Do the same thing with the second toy you brought, and progress all the way down to your fifth and final item.

By now, you will have an idea of which ones he likes best, so pick up two of the toys your dog was least interested in and repeat the playing game. Which one does your dog like the best? Which is he looking at, and which one does he sniff and nudge you to get at? Put them both on the floor, and see which one he picks up first. The toy he is interested in will be number four on your list, and the one he left on the floor is number five. Do the same things with the others until you can make a list in order of your dog's favourite items of interaction. AKA toys!

My dog's five favourite toys:

1)

2)

3)

4)

5)

The order may change slightly as you go through the audit, but don't worry about that; just take your time and enjoy the process. This isn't just an exercise to do once; practise it a couple of times over a few days, and observe your dog all the time. Is he looking at you ever or always the toy? Does he try and get it off you by sitting or barking or giving you his paw? Can you make something from the bottom of the list more desirable by changing the tone of your voice? If you go squeaky, does he get more excited? Even after a short while playing this, something will become apparent, and that is it's not about the toy; it's what we do with it that matters.

Remember though – information doesn't equal transformation; action does! You are not going to get your dog to love you any more or want to be with you by reading and thinking about it, so have some fun playing with your dog and practise playing with your dog.

So you have officially begun your dog audit, and already you have a very clear idea of the type of toys your dog likes playing with. Well done.

Touch

So while we have our dog's attention, we are going to build on this and continue finding out where our dog likes to be touched and stroked. Why is this important? Well, lots of reasons. Stroking and grooming can be your dog's daily health check. You can check for cuts, bruises, or any lumps he may have, but mainly it's because our dogs enjoy it, and it's good for us too. Stroking a dog has been medically proven to reduce heart rate and stress, so do it daily and consider it a reward to yourself and an important part of your daily routine, just like having a meal with your family or doing some exercise.

So touching and stroking your dog is not only good for you, but he should enjoy it as well. Maybe not so much at first, but the more you do it, the more pleasurable he will find it. And it will also help with your training too. What if having his butt scratched was one of your dog's top three things in the world. Wouldn't you like to know that information so you could use it? You betcha you would, so let's do it. You are probably best doing this exercise after a walk so your dog has less energy and the stroking doesn't get him so excited that he starts jumping all over you. Or you can do as I just suggested and start the affection section after you have done the toy audit.

Exercise:

Start by talking to your dog and give him a stroke on his head. Then move down his back and try his ears next. Which area does he lean into and close his eyes with pleasure? He may even offer a little blissful groan. That's your number one on the list. Now just go round his body slowly and talk to him and see where you think the other four places are. To rank them in order of pleasure, you could try stroking and talking to him in one position and see how long it takes him to get bored. Then start somewhere else. There's no real science to this; it's mainly trial and error. Once again your dog may be thinking 'What's this all about then? This only normally happens on a Saturday evening.'

Your success with this task will depend in part on how much your dog was handled as a puppy. Dogs that have enjoyed being stroked as a puppy will enjoy this more. Some dogs are less keen to be touched in certain places, and certainly the feet, ears, and bum can be areas your dog may feel uncomfortable with you touching. That's why it's important to take your time and talk to your dog. Don't force yourself on him. You want to know what he enjoys and loves, so listen to him, and that means avoid anything that makes him uncomfortable for now.

Repeat this exercise a couple of times, and then rank the top five places your dog likes to be touched in order.

My dog's five favourite touch points:

1)

2)

3)

4)

5)

Now we can move onto food, yummy yummy.

Food

Food is great. I love it and so do my dogs, but if we are being honest, we kind of know our dogs like food, so that's why we do toys and touch first. Also, what happens if you just train your dog with food, and one day in the park you shout at him to come back and he isn't hungry? That's the thing with just using food to train your dog; it can make you lazy. You can lose some of the connection with your dog and just end up becoming a treat dispenser for him. Remember; when using food, we want just as much animation as we did with the toys, so really try and make the food come alive. Remember your dog is quite selfish, and he likes stuff other people are enjoying, so you should make a big fuss about the food, especially when you are using the lower-value treats.

Exercise:

Get your five or six different treats and see which one he likes best. I would suggest putting a very small amount into five cups or bowls and taking each one out in turn. This game is somewhat easier as the dogs are generally more motivated, but you still need to have that conversation with your dog where you say 'Oh, what's this! Look what have I got here, a piece of cheese and a piece of ham. Which one do you like best, my lovely little doggy?' Then take one of each type of food and cup in each hand, put them both under his nose, separate your hands, and see which one his nose follows. Repeat four or five times.

Remember the point of the audit is for you to find five options for each section in a minute, but your training won't be as effective if you just guess. You may be able to tell me after thinking about it for a minute that your dog's top thing in each list is a tennis ball, being stroked behind his ears, and liver treats, but that's not really the point. I want you to get to know your dog a little deeper than that. Once we have all the knowledge, then playing and training become so much easier, so let's get all the tools we need first.

Gradually work your way through the rest of the food-stuffs until you have a list of the ones he liked in order of preference.

My dog's favourite foods:

1)

2)

3)

4)

5)

People

Next, we want to find out your dog's five favourite people. Obviously, if you live alone with your dog, I'm not suggesting you get married and adopt three children just to do this exercise. Although don't let me stop you either.

No, this is more if you have a family or a regular circle of friends your dog usually sees. The easiest way to see which family member your dog likes would be for you all to go off to the park, where one of you holds the dog on his lead while the others walk a short distance away. Then you let go of the lead while they all encourage the dog to come towards them. The one the dog goes to is the one he likes best. Don't get upset with me if when you try this, it wasn't you that your dog went to; the dog won't lie.

If the park is too distracting for your dog at the moment, then do the exercise in the house or garden. But don't use food or toys to tempt him in this exercise. We want to know which person he actually likes.

My dog's favourite people:

1)

2)

3)

4)

5)

Places

Next, we have the five most stimulating places you take your dog. If you are self-isolating, then I'm not suggesting you both go and drive around your town jumping in and out of the car at various locations, so this is one section you can probably do from the comfort of your own chair.

Knowing where the most stimulating places your dog visits is going to help you once your self-isolation is over. And, depending on how well-travelled your dog is, you may have a list of places that is longer than five…

Think about all the places you take your dog and how much he enjoys each place. I would like you to rank these, starting with the place where your dog is most excitable, and you have the least control over him. You can go into more detail here too because there will be environmental factors that will change things; for example, the list may look like this:

1. Wherever we are when he sees another dog
2. The beach when the tide is out

3. Grandma's house when all the nephews and nieces are there
4. The woods when the pheasants are out
5. When we walk past the scrapyard and he barks at that Doberman he doesn't like

You get the idea.

Now if you went on down the list of every location your dog has ever been to, then after a few hours you would hopefully end up with your sitting room, living room, or elsewhere in your house at the end because your house is likely to be the least stimulating. It's where he spends most of his resting time, and apart from his toys, he has long ago finished being interested in any of the items in the room.

This is convenient for you because this is exactly where you are going to start playing with and training your dog.

What to play with and how to play with your dog

Up to now, I have described how you can start interacting with your dog to test and explore which toys and treats he likes, and I said you should play with your dog as if you are five years old, without any inhibitions or cares in the world. You need to be silly and a bit goofy, make lots of stupid noises and do whatever it takes to get your dog to look at you and wag his tail. Basically, I want you to 'be more dog'!

Think back to when you have seen two playful dogs meeting up in the park off lead. They slowly approach each other maintaining eye contact until they are both standing quite still, with maybe a rather stiff wag of the tail. Then, after a few seconds, one of them will jump into a little crouch position with his head down slightly, at which point the other dog will tense up, and they will begin to chase each other around. This may be the point where you lose control of your dog. Hopefully, by now you have realised it's not a very good idea for you to allow your dog to think playing with other dogs is the best thing since sliced bread. Not if you want to enjoy stress-free trips to the park anyway.

Just before the dogs run off together, one of the dogs does a little jump into a crouch, which says to the other dog 'You wanna play? OK, chase me!' That is what you are up against when you go to the park. That's what I need you to recreate with your dog now. I'm not suggesting you take your dog to the park and attempt to get him to chase you there, but I do want you to 'be more dog'.

This can be quite hard at first because for some of us, it's been a long time since we were children. We might have forgotten how to play and be silly. But you just have to try, and don't be afraid of messing up. You can be really interesting to your dog, but he just doesn't know it yet. Interaction or playing with your dog is like going to the gym and using a muscle that you haven't used for a while. It's really hard at first. It feels awkward and you might feel like quitting, but don't. Once you get past that awkward stage, things get a little easier, and pretty soon you will start lifting heavier weights and feeling fitter and experiencing all the awesome feelings that come with that.

You are reading this because you want your dog not to run away or pull on the lead, or you want him to be more obedient. Well, you first need him to be more interested in you, and we do that by teaching him that actually, you are a fun person to be with. If you do nothing else but start playing with your dog regularly as I have described, you will build a great relationship with him, and your whole life with your dog will be much more enjoyable.

You will be a better owner too, one who knows what his dog likes, and eventually, you will have much more control on walks because you will have what my good friend David Davies calls the invisible leash. This is where you are connected by more than just a physical lead, and your dog comes back to you and stays near you because he wants to be with you rather than because you restrained him or are shouting at him.

So playing with a toy involves you choosing a toy (or thing) and you getting on the floor and playing with him.

Exercise: Playing with toys

Start at home in your front room or somewhere with low distractions, and you will be less self-conscious.

Take the item that became Kryptonite number five on the list of your dog's favourite items. Before you begin this game, try and have two of the items and make sure they are almost identical, so two socks or hairbrushes or two balls, etc.

Then get your dog's attention (say his name in a cheery voice), and when he looks at you, start talking to him about this wonderful toy, much as you did when you were finding the Kryptonite earlier in the chapter. Keep talking, and you will gradually build his interest and desire to get the toy, but don't give it to him yet. Tease him a little with it if you have to, but remember not to do this if he is normally in any way possessive over a toy as this will just piss him off. Speak in a high-pitched voice, and see what he reacts to. Then when he does something like come towards you, sit in front of you, or even just look at you, show him the toy and see how he reacts.

Does he want it very badly? Is he whining or pawing at you, is he wagging his tail, and does he look happy? Can you make him any more interested by talking to him and telling him how awesome the toy is?

You are basically looking for some kind of reaction from your dog that you wouldn't normally have got. If at this point you normally just throw your toy for your dog, then this time maybe wait a while for him to sit or give you eye contact. It's at that moment you can tell him what a good boy he is and share the toy with him. If he doesn't do anything, then maybe move the toy around, and see if by moving it above his head, you can 'lure' him into a 'sit'. (Basically by just using the toy and your encouraging voice, what can you get him to do for you?) You are not allowed to say 'Sit' yet even if he knows that command.

If you find yourself in a position where you get no reaction at all from your dog, then you need to work a bit harder; maybe get on the floor with him, make the toy move around on the floor, and encourage your dog to chase it. These toys have been ranked in order of how much your dog likes them, so play or interaction time should be quite easy. Your dog may not, however, associate you with the fun of the toy, so keep working hard to get his interest. You are trying to convince the dog that playing a game with you and the toy is more fun than him having the toy to himself.

Of course, he could just be having an off day, so don't stress too much if nothing happens; you can just try again tomorrow. In the meantime, make sure you don't leave the play toys lying around on the floor, and put them away. You could carry one around the house with you, or play a game of pass with your partner; then when the dog shows an interest, you can put the thing away. Do this a few times, and you should soon build some desire for the thing you want to use.

This play or interacting is the start of you connecting with your dog. It's very important for a number of reasons.

By controlling all of the things your dog likes all of a sudden, you instantly raise your status in his eyes, and you become more interesting to him just by association.

By playing and talking, you are actually teaching him your language. You will pick up bits of your dog's body language too, but it's more important that he knows your language and what you want from him. So by doing very basic things such as showing him a toy (something he likes) and getting him to do something (eye contact or a 'sit') and then rewarding him, you are showing him what he needs to do to get a reward (the thing he wants).

It's also great fun! For many of the people within my Superhero Dog Owners Inner Circle, the dog audit is the turning point in their relationship with their dogs. This is where they realise their dogs will listen to them and do what they want, even if it's just giving eye contact for one of their favourite toys.

So once you have some focus and reaction, you can continue, and there are two great games you can also play. The first is two toys…

The game of two toys

The basic premise of two toys is you have two toys (or two hairbrushes or plastic bottles or whatever it is that was on the list of things your dog loved). The toys should be almost identical, otherwise the dog will prefer one over the other. First, get your dog interested in one of the toys; then throw or drop the toy a short distance away. When he goes off to see what you have thrown, take out the second toy and start getting him interested in that. Dogs usually want what someone else has got, so you can make your toy seem more interesting by using your voice and the way you act. Say your dog's name in a nice cheery voice. Move away from him with it slightly and he may follow; then keep talking to your toy, throw it up and catch it, and make stupid noises, 'Whoop whoop!'

The moment your dog drops the first toy, you can drop or throw the one you are holding for him, and then you pick up the first one and start the process again. Try and drop the second toy on the other side of where you dropped the first. If you make yourself the centre of the game with toys being dropped either side of where you are standing, you will be able to retrieve the dropped toys and control the game better.

This is all rather high energy, and dogs really love it. It's very important you don't try and take the toy from the dog, but rather wait for him to drop it. That way he learns when he drops a toy he actually gets another one, so this game is going to teach him that he doesn't need to run off with things, and it's better to share them with you.

You should be talking to your dog and praising him the whole time, especially when he drops the toy and comes towards you for the toy you are holding.

If you are really struggling to get your dog to drop the first toy you threw, then use one of the more desirable items of Kryptonite from the list. You know he likes a number two or three toy more than a five, so use it. See, there is a method in my madness.

The second game is tuggy tugg tugg.

Tuggy tugg tugg

Once again, you shouldn't play this game if your dog is normally possessive over his toys, but most dogs will be fine with it.

You can play tuggy with anything at all that both you and your dog can safely hold, but it's easier if it's a cloth or rope-type material. An old towel or tea towel cut into one- to two-foot long strips with a knot at each end does the job perfectly. I have never met a dog yet who refused to play a game with me because I wasn't using a branded dog toy…

So first get the toy and make it 'come alive', much the same as you did for the other game, only this time you are going to encourage your dog to get hold of it. Don't try and force the toy on him, or he will likely back away from you. You can throw it a short distance or run with it or make it move around the floor and encourage your dog to 'get it'.

You should be telling your dog he is a 'Good boy' every time he looks interested or moves towards the toy and also if he attempts to mouth it.

When he does finally hold the toy, tell him he is a 'Good boy' and have a short game of tuggy. You need to judge this as you play, but don't be too physical at first, and when your dog gets into it, just stop moving the toy. Keep your arm still and wait for him to let go. And wait and wait. You may have to put two hands on the toy (one on either end of the toy with your dog's grip in the middle). Then, and this is the important bit, when he does let go, tell him in a very cheery voice that he's a good boy! And give him his end of the toy straight back again and have another short game of tuggy. Continue this five or six times and then stop. Go and make yourself a brew as a reward and have a sit-down and think about what you did. Your dog can enjoy a biscuit at the same time.

Remember the idea is you are teaching the dog that it's more fun to play with you than it is to keep, run off with, and chew up the toy. So you need to teach him that the game does not end when the pulling and letting go stops, and it will start back up again. Obviously, the game has to end sometime, and when it does, you can just tell your dog he is a very good boy and give him some affection. Leaving him wanting more isn't a bad thing.

You should play this game little and often, and always remember to put the toy away when you are finished playing. Don't fall into the trap of telling your dog to 'LEAVE IT' every two seconds, much better to just wait until he lets go. If you really struggle to get him to leave it, exchange a treat for the toy and then resume the game.

And that's tuggy tugg tugg. It's a great physical game, which most dogs really love. Unlike a retrieving game, it keeps your dog near you all the time, and for dogs that really enjoy playing, it can be a great high-energy reward for doing something they like.

Be careful if you are playing this game with puppies – if you are too vigorous, you can easily pull their teeth out. Also, when you are playing tuggy, try and use a forward-and-back motion rather than side to side, as playing tuggy with a side-to-side action can mimic a killing action for a dog.

So this has been a busy old chapter. By now you should have a list of toys your dog likes playing with, his favourite foods, where he likes to be touched and stroked, his five favourite people in the world, and the five most stimulating locations. You also know how to use the Kryptonite to play and interact with your dog.

Here is a checklist once again for your dog audit:

- Find your dog's Kryptonite
- Keep it special
- Start playing with your dog somewhere with low distractions
- Play with your dog little and often
- Enjoy it!

Don't be afraid to screw up, ever!

Final exercise:

You MUST do this exercise because it is very powerful and will save you untold heartache later on. Sometime today I want you to pick one of your dog's less desirable items of Kryptonite, such as his number-five toy or food item. Then I want you to go outside into your garden or yard and try and play the same game with your dog. Use the exact same technique you did indoors and just play with him. As you are playing, watch your dog to see if he acts any differently to when he was indoors. Do this today, and we will come back to this a little later.

Who's a good boy?

You won't hear this on dog training courses or read it anywhere else, but walking and exercising your dog can be a real pain in the arse, can't it? All that pulling on the lead really hurts, and when he ignores you when you let him off lead, it's rather embarrassing too. I used to find it really tiring, and I'm sure my dog didn't enjoy it very much either. Day after day I would come home after a walk sick of the sound of my own voice telling my dog off all the time, 'Come back', 'Get back', 'Leave that', Leave him', 'Get down', etc. Well, if you have ever felt like that too, then this chapter shows you how you can change all of that and start enjoying your dog again.

If you look back through this chapter and count up how many times I said talk to your dog in a cheery voice and tell him he's a good boy, you would count five. Basically, every time he does something you want, you need to tell him he is a good boy.

Playing with your dog this way is going to make you both much happier, and owning a dog will be much less stressful. Yes, we have a long way to go with the training, but let's start by enjoying ourselves a bit.

So who is a good boy? Well, tell him, and then he will know. Your dog will like being a good boy, and if it's pleasurable enough for him, he will want to do whatever it takes to be a good boy to get the reward from you.

So that is the first stage of the dog audit done. If you have done this correctly and have a list of things your dog loves, then you probably know more about your dog than 80% of the dog owners on the planet.

If you haven't, then go back and do it again. Trust me, just doing this audit and going through the play-with-your-dog process will profoundly change your life. Your dog will look at you differently now: with respect and interest. After all, you control the good things in life, so why wouldn't he be more interested in you?

So what now? Well, you can stay at this stage for a little or a lot longer and just enjoy your dog at home where it's safe. But if you want to enjoy that same kind of playing experience with your dog outside, then we need to take it up a notch and start getting your dog to earn the rewards he so loves. And we do that by attempting a little thing called dog training… you may have heard of it.

Now, this isn't the bit where you put the book down because it's too complicated and you think you won't be able to train your dog: far from it! You have been teaching your dog already by teaching him to play with you, so this follows on nicely. In any case, we are going to train with my unique spin, so you and your dog are guaranteed to enjoy it.

Chapter summary

- Using the toys, treats, and other things your dog likes will give you an easy way to start bonding with him. But don't expect him to start doing backflips or rollovers just because you are holding his favourite toy. How interesting your dog finds you and your relationship with him will improve over time, so keep at it with the games, and treat any increased interest from him as a small success.
- Don't just shove the treat or toy in your dog's face, or he may back away. Far better to tease your dog and try and make him come towards you. Most dogs will chase things that move, so use the different items of Kryptonite to 'be more dog' and encourage him to move. With some hard work, pretty soon you will have a remote-controlled dog that you can make do all kinds of things using all the resources you discover when you do your dog audit.
- This is the moment in the book when you go from learning how to play with and train your dog to *actually* playing with and training him. You should be looking forward to this because you will thoroughly enjoy find-

ing out what your dog likes. Remember, action equals transformation, so get on the floor and play. The more you play and convince your dog that you are an awesome person, the easier it will be to fix the bad behaviours you don't want him to exhibit.

What to teach your dog

When you think of dog training, you may have visions of a sergeant-major-type character who shows you how to march around a field anticlockwise with your dog marking out a perfect square (because that's normal, isn't it?). And you must always set off on the left foot first (like the dog gives a shit which foot you set off on). And if he strays slightly forward, you must say HEEL DOG and pull him towards you (because that will make him want to do it, won't it?)

Of course, not all dog-training classes are like that, but they do exist. I know some amazing dog trainers who run fantastic classes where you learn new things together that help you improve the relationship between you and your dog. But some of them teach the most pointless exercises that do nothing to help an owner get their dog more interested in them and have little value to anyone who lives in the real world.

I would also avoid any training class where the dogs or puppies are encouraged to have 10 minutes' 'free play'. It's likely that this free play will be the one thing your dog will enjoy the most AND remember from the class, and so will be the one thing he wants to do again when he sees another dog.

The best advice would be to go along to a class BEFORE you get your puppy or dog and see exactly what is taught. You need to question whether the class will help you teach your dog that you're the most interesting thing in his world and make him easier to walk and live with.

At the time of writing, this going to a puppy class might not even be an option, but there are a lot of dog trainers offering 'online puppy classes' and I've also written a book called *The Perfect Puppy Project* which will show you how to 'home-school' your puppy.

So, I personally like to teach my dogs stuff to do that is going to keep them close to me and make them want to be with me. And we are going to start with your dog's name.

What does your dog's name mean to him?

"It ain't what they call you; it's what you answer to."
— W.C. Fields

I think the most important thing you will ever teach your dog is his name and that saying his name means he should either look at you or come to you. Some trainers will say that a 'stop' command or a 'leave it' is more important, but I think it will help you most if you teach your dog to enjoy being with you all of the time. We are going to start that by making your dog think that something awesome is going to come from you whenever he hears his name.

I like my dog to associate hearing his name with a recall because whether you like it or not, your dog's name is the thing you usually say when you want them to come.

That's why we started the eye contact exercise in chapter 1. Rewarding your dog with a smile, a 'good boy' or a pat on the head (or even all three) every time he gives you eye contact is going to build up a great association in his mind of why he should look at you when he hears his name. You should continue to reward eye contact as often as you can to build on this. Turn every meal or treat time into an opportunity to further practise focusing on eye contact.

Exercise: 'Watch me'

Next time you go to give your dog a treat, say his name and wait for him to give you eye contact before you give it to him. This may take a while at first because he may be focused on the treat, so be patient. As soon as his eyes hit yours, say, 'Good boy'. When he is doing it regularly, you can start to say 'Watch me' or 'Watch' or whatever you prefer. You can practise this further at meal times and ask your dog to 'Watch me' before you feed him. You could be extra smart and split the meal into five portions and practise a 'Watch me' before you feed him each bowl. This is the little-and-often way of training your dog, and it's one I prefer. Far better to make playing and interacting with your dog and training and challenging him part of your everyday routine than embarking on some intensive and serious training session where you put too much pressure on yourself to succeed. It's like the benefits of eating healthily all year round, rather than losing 10 pounds in a two-week crash diet where you inevitably end up back where you started.

Once you are having regular success with the 'Watch me' exercise, you should develop it into a 'catch-up' game.

The catch-up game

This game can be played with food or toys as well as affection, and it puts the emphasis on your dog being rewarded for coming to you. This enables you to practise a recall many times every day, in your home and garden.

By now, your dog should be responding well when he hears his name called by you. Dogs love attention, and if the consequence of him giving you his attention is rewarded regularly, then he will do it more often. Not only that, he will want to do it and should start following you more because he associates being with you as enjoyable.

You should use low-value treats for this exercise, such as a number four or five from the list you made earlier in your dog audit. Similarly use a low-value toy, preferably two that are identical. Of course, if you have been practising or if your dog is responding well to the sound of your voice, then don't use any toys at all; just use affection and praise.

Let's assume you have a bowl of your dog's mixer to hand. Take a small handful and show your dog one of the pieces, then throw the treat a metre or two away, but so your dog sees it being thrown. Your dog should go and retrieve the treat from the floor. Then just as he eats it, call his name in your happy dog voice, and as he comes towards you, wave another treat at him. As he gets near to you, throw that treat to the side of you that's furthest away from the direction he is coming from. Again, not too far away, you want him to get the reward. As soon as he collects that treat or toy, you should call his name again. As he gets quicker, you can increase the distance you throw the treat. Also, as he is retrieving the treat, you can walk in the opposite direction, so he has a bit further to come to you.

When your dog has the idea, you can start mixing it up a bit. Every third or fourth go, don't throw a treat, and instead, when he gets to you praise him, stroke his ears and tell him what a brilliant dog he is. Then start the game again, and this time on the third go, when he is retrieving the thrown treat, say his name, and when he comes towards you, have three treats ready in your hand to reward him with. Dogs are eternal chancers, and mixing up the rewards like this will keep him guessing as to what he is going to get next.

This game can then be taken into the garden, and it's a good game to play in the park with your dog on a long lead if you wish. Remember, you may need to use a higher-value item of Kryptonite when you are exercising somewhere with more distractions.

The 'Watch me' and 'catch-up' games are games you can and should play whenever you feed or play with your dog.

You can't ban the fun, so be the fun instead

From 1920 to 1933, prohibition was in effect throughout the United States of America. However, the government struggled to enforce the legislation, which banned the manufacture, transportation, and sale of intoxicating liquor. This was just as well because a large portion of the population across all classes of society enjoyed a drink. Actually drinking alcohol wasn't illegal, so drink it they continued to do. They sometimes made do with moonshine or homemade bathtub gin or more usually enjoyed the whisky and rum that flowed in illegal speakeasies right across the country. The point is you can't just ban something that people enjoy and expect them not to find another way to get what they want.

And so it is with your dog. You have identified all the places and triggers that cause your dog to be badly behaved, and hopefully I have convinced you by now that if you want to improve your dog's behaviour, then you need to start doing something different. We already know that play, interaction, and challenge are key daily needs that require fulfilling for our dogs, so if we are going to stop them from having fun one way, we need to replace that with another kind of fun. And that is having fun with us.

Many training clients begin the process of bonding and playing with and training their dog, but then too quickly, they rush off to the park to see if their dog's behaviour is any better. My advice to you is **not to do that** as inevitably your dog will quickly revert back to the bad behaviour he used to exhibit in that place. To see a lasting change in your dog, you need to completely avoid where he is naughty for around a month or so; six weeks would be even better.

If you had a sharp intake of breath at my suggestion that you don't go to the park for six weeks, then hear me out. This is going to be easier than you think, and there are three good reasons why you should follow my plan.

1) It works. Yes, it really does. If you were having a training consultation with me in person, the first thing I would do would be to identify the problem and advise you to avoid it completely where possible. Then we would begin teaching your dog something new to do instead.

2) Avoiding the thing your dog doesn't like makes it much easier for you to teach him something new. If he's distracted, then you won't have his attention, and without his attention, you might as well not bother. Then you will get frustrated at your dog and end up feeling like a failure. To avoid this and make it as easy as possible for your dog to associate being with **you** with having fun, you should remove anything else he may find interesting. This doesn't completely solve the problem, but it makes it a lot more likely you will succeed. Think of it like starting a diet. The chances of you snacking on some strawberries when you feel a little peckish rather than p-p-picking up a Penguin will be much greater if you have stocked up on some ripe and tasty fruits and thrown away all of the biscuits before you start.

3) Your life will be better. Yes, that is a lofty claim for a dog walker from Sunderland to make, but it's true. By following this plan, you will remove lots of stress from your life almost overnight.

Think of it like trying to lose weight, which is something that I struggle with from time to time. You start by seeing what weight you are and decide on a target weight. Then you might join a gym, start running or follow a training plan, which will help you gradually move towards your target weight. But the training is just part of the equation because if you continue to sneak a chocolate bar or a slice of pizza every day, you sabotage your chances of getting to your target weight. You may still lose some, but you don't ever end up getting the result you wanted at the start.

This does require a small shift in mindset from you. Start thinking of your dog as someone that needs safety, exercise, interaction, and challenge in his life rather than a walk to the park. If all he does is misbehave and stress you out at the park, then this period of self-isolation is a great opportunity for your dog to go 'cold turkey' on all the naughty things he does at the park.

So what will you do instead?

Well, that's what we will find out in the next chapter.

Chapter summary

- It's vital to ensure that your dog's learning environment is as distraction-free as possible. I remember when I was in a science class at school and there were a couple of pigeons screwing on the roof opposite; I couldn't concentrate for love nor money. Well, your dog will be as easily distracted as I was by anything that moves, not to mention any smells, which obviously you can't see. So play with him and train him somewhere quiet, or better still, stay at home.

- Think about your dog's name and more importantly, what he thinks of when he hears his name. If he associates his name with a pleasant experience, then he will come to you and listen to you quickly, which will make controlling him much easier. Get in the habit of rewarding eye contact often, and especially reward him when he offers you eye contact of his own accord. If your dog regularly checks in with you, it will make for stress-free walks.
- When it comes to what you actually train your dog to do, the list is varied and almost endless. Not everything I teach in the book will work with every dog, but there are games, tricks, and exercises to suit any dog, so try everything at least once. I like to play games that keep my dogs close by me and you should too because that way your walks will be safer and eventually you will be able to exercise your dog anywhere off lead. This is the nirvana for all dog owners.

Chapter Two

The Hungry Games

"Hounds follow those who feed them."
– Otto von Bismarck

I have dedicated this short chapter exclusively to your dog's food because it's a very precious resource that most dog owners can use more effectively, to make living with their dogs much easier. Let's find out why…

Go back in time by around 30,000 years to when men lived in caves. Let's imagine that over a particular few days, a tribe successfully hunted a mammoth. They used almost all parts of the mammoth, but there were still a few pieces left over. On the outskirts of a cave, there were some wild dogs or wolves who had been taking a keen interest in the goings-on at the cave. Some of them had been venturing closer to the humans and occasionally were rewarded with some scraps.

Now expert opinion differs on how exactly humans and wolves came together, but it isn't hard to imagine a scenario where man may have come upon a stray or abandoned wolf cub and raised it within his family. This semi-domesticated wolf would in time have taken a place at the hearth and taken on the role of hunter and guarder as well as companion, but it was food that brought man and wolf together.

You should know by now that I am a huge fan of training your dog through play and interaction, using toys and affection to help you bond with him and reward him. I go on about playing with your dog because most dogs just love playing; they crave attention, excitement, and entertainment, and if we don't provide it, then they will find it elsewhere.

You certainly won't be as important to your dog if you just use food to train him. What happens if you just train with food, and one day at the park your little Schnauzer finds a scent that leads him to a rather attractive female, and before you know it, the dogs are frolicking around like a scene from *Lady and the Tramp*? You try and call him over and stand with your bit of cheese, but your dog thinks 'Actually, I'm not hungry, Dad. You can have that bit. I will stay here.'

It's a much better idea to have your dog think you are an exciting person to be with rather than just a food dispenser. Think of it as you providing dinner and a show rather than just a pizza takeout.

You should try and inject lots of emotion into your training even when you are using treats. Dogs love attention, and by giving your dog a smile and a stroke and telling him he is a good boy, you are giving him a much more personal reward than just the treat. Training this way will mean that in time you may be able to phase the treats out and just use your voice and your affection as rewards for your dog.

All that aside, it has to be said that for most dogs, food is their number-one pleasure. And there are ways you can use your dog's food a lot better than just feeding two meals a day and a few treats. And if you currently just leave your dog's food down all day for him to graze on, then in my humble and correct opinion, this is a waste of what for many dogs is their most precious resource. Think back to when you did the dog audit, and I recommended that you stopped leaving your dog's favourite toys lying around the house and kept them for when you were playing with him. It's a similar thing with the food. You won't be able to get your dog to work for his food if it's a free resource he can have whenever he wants.

If there were bags of money in the foyer of your office block that you were allowed to help yourself to on a Monday morning, would you walk past them and still go to work, or just help yourself and blow off the pointless task of actually earning it?

We have already discussed using food to teach your dog tricks, and if you are struggling to get your dog interested in a toy, then using food to play with, train, and entertain your dog may be your only option. It's worth stressing that if you are going to use food, you should only use the regular amount of food your dog eats throughout the day and not just feed more when you do any training with him. If you have to use a higher-value treat, then be aware of how many calories that treat will have, and adjust your dog's daily food intake accordingly.

This is even more important when you are self-isolating, and your dog isn't getting his usual level of exercise. The last thing you want is for your dog to gain weight and come out of a period of self-isolation with underlying, or extreme health problems that could have been avoided if you had fed him the appropriate amount of food that matched his exercise needs at the time.

You can get more out of your dog's daily intake by spreading his food out into several portions, but don't start taking food away from your dog and putting him in a situation where he feels like he has to defend his food.

Far better for your dog to see you as the giver of food and the provider of nice things that he likes, and leave any macho food-bowl standoffs for dog whisperers who enjoy being bitten.

So instead of giving your dog his whole breakfast or tea in one bowl, you could split it into five portions and use it as a reward for a simple recall exercise; you can put a small amount of food into your dog's bowl then walk away from him, and when he is finished, call him to you in a nice cheery voice and reward him with a handful of meal. Repeat this four or five times, always being sure to supplement the giving of the food with praise and affection.

I split my own dogs' daily ration of food and treats into thirds. One third is split between two small meals, one in the morning and one in the evening.

The second portion is spread throughout the day and fed by hand in various games and training exercises – some goes in my coat pocket to use when I'm at the park, and some is placed in a bowl that goes on my mantlepiece to use indoors either as part of training or just to reinforce any good behaviour my dogs might exhibit throughout the day.

The final third I use in food dispensers, which entertain my dogs throughout the day when I am busy doing other things. Depending on how busy I am, I may even split the whole day's ration so I train with half of it and the rest will go in food dispensing toys. I am going to go into the wonderful world of food dispensing toys next, but see how I use my dog's food throughout the whole day to train, entertain, and challenge him. Would your dog enjoy his food a little more if he has to earn it rather than just be given it as one or two meals to graze on whenever he pleases?

You betcha, he would!

So, let's look at some simple food games that will entertain your dog while he is eating.

Food games

Dogs rarely seem to get bored when it comes to finding food, and if you wish, you should be able to get your dog to find a whole bowl's worth of kibble even if it's fed in individual pieces. You can play 'find it' games with your dog's food in your house, hiding pieces under upturned cups, or from one room to another, outside in the garden, and even in your local park. Be careful outside that your dog doesn't leave any treats behind or eat anything else that could be dangerous for him. The instructions for teaching a 'find it' game can be found in chapter 5.

You also have the 'leave it' and the 'catch up' games that you should use to mentally and physically tire your dog out. However, there is another way you can challenge your dog further with food, even when you are not at home.

King KONG

Most dog owners I meet own a KONG toy, but few use them to their full potential. In case you live on the moon, KONGs are funny-shaped food dispensers that are made from super-tough rubber. Most dogs struggle to chew them to pieces, which makes them incredibly safe and perfect for putting food in. The standard one is the red KONG, but there is also a black version, which is even tougher for dogs with super-strong jaws. There are also softer puppy KONGs and a purple version for older dogs whose jaws may not be so strong. I also own a number of **Planet Dog** treat dispensers too, and my dogs have lots of fun with both.

There are also **Licky Mats**, on which you can spread some peanut butter, fruit or leftover gravy (depending on what your dog likes.)

Snufflemats are also a fabulous way to make your dog's food last longer. They are mats that allow the dogs to find dry food or treats that you've hidden. So, you're feeding your dog while also letting their brain be stimulated as they savour and sniff out their food. It turns feeding time into a stimulating activity. (Not suitable for raw food)

There are some homemade easy-options too.

Instead of a Snuffle mat, you could hide your dog's dried treats and kibble in a pile of cloth you've made out of old clothes, socks, towels or ripped up cardboard boxes.

And instead of a Kong, you could of course just use an empty milk or orange carton. Rinse it out, throw the top away and fill with some treats or kibble and give to your dog. He will probably have great fun exploring how to get the food out of it. My Bordeaux Barry used to love this game. He seems to really enjoy ripping up boxes, and he has become quite the expert at it too.

The problem with using something homemade is you really need to observe your dog all the time in case he rips off a piece of cardboard or worse, plastic, and tries to eat it. This should be less of a problem if you are with your dog self-isolating.

That's why I recommend buying several food dispensing toys that have been made for dogs. There are loads on the market to choose from; the ones above are just my personal favourites. More important than the treat dispenser is you actually using it. Dogs love sniffing, licking, and chewing, so by providing them with a suitable toy crammed with food, you are providing an outlet and a further challenge that you can build into your dog's daily routine.

There are a million ways to fill a treat dispenser, and as you already know your dog's five favourite foods, you should have no trouble filling one to your dog's satisfaction. You can fill the toy with 10% favourite treat and 90% regular kibble, and your dog will still love the KONG.

The challenge of getting to the tasty stuff inside will bring him a lot of joy, so be creative with what you put inside the treat dispenser. If you don't have one, then go and buy one, and if you already have one, then get a different kind. Providing you wash them between uses, you can use them over and over again, so they are great value for money, and if your dog could, then he would thank you for it too.

Chapter summary

- There are a number of dog trainers out there who would have you believe you shouldn't just use food when you are training a dog. I agree with that. You should always use emotion and praise <u>in addition</u> to the food you are using to reward your dog. Food rates pretty high on most dogs' wish list, so you would be silly not to use it.
- Use it all throughout the day too. Use it to practise tricks or retrieves or 'find it' games. Use it in KONGs as often as your dog will eat from them, and if he loves his food, then he will love eating his food from a treat dispenser like a KONG. Feeding your dog like this is a very easy way to put a daily challenge into his routine.
- Remember one bowl of food can be 50 tricks, 20 re-calls, 10 KONGs or 30 minutes playing 'find it' in the garden, home, or wherever you take the time to hide the food. That bowl of food sounds pretty boring in comparison now, doesn't it? If you agree, then go into

the kitchen now, throw away the bowl, and for dog's sake, use the food!

Chapter Three

Using Food to Change your Dog's Bad Habits

"Scratch a dog and you'll find a permanent job"
Franklin P. Jones

One huge mistake we made with our first dog, Flo, was not getting her used to being handled by humans. She was a nine-week-old ratbag when we rescued her from the kennels, and she remained much the same for the next 14 years. That's not strictly true as she became, in my eyes, the model dog for the last six years of her life.

But her early weeks had obviously been quite stressful and unsettled, and because of that, she was quite a wild and feral puppy.

That's only one side of the story though, and I represented the other half of the equation. And I made the most fatal of errors which many new puppy owners make … I got a dog when I knew diddly-squat about dogs!

Flo was a terror, and *I* was an idiot. Not a great combination.

My wife had grown up with Staffies her whole life, but Flo was a challenge even for her.

We struggled through the entire puppyhood phase, and this wasn't made any easier by the fact we actually acquired the dog two weeks after we moved into our first home, with a six-month-old baby in tow.

Like I said, not a good recipe for success.

The sad thing is I know I could have drastically improved Flo's behaviour and moulded her into a much easier-to-manage dog if I'd known the contents of this chapter.

Hindsight is a wonderful thing, and there are lots of things I would have done differently if I could have my time with her again.

At the top of the list of things would be to teach her to not be afraid of being handled and touched. But because, at the time, I didn't teach my dog handling skills, I ended up enduring miserable vet's visits for Flo's entire life.

She simply hated being touched anywhere on her body. Bandaging a cut paw of hers was a test of strength and endurance, and even just a regular vet's check-up would mean I had to clamp my hands around her jaws and hold her still while the vet checked her over.

It upsets me to think about this, let alone write about it, but when the time came for Flo to be put to sleep at the vet's, despite being old, weak and slightly delirious because of the epilepsy she was suffering from, I still had to hold her down firmly while the vet administered the drug that would sadly end her life.

Losing a dog is never a nice moment, but those final minutes with Flo could have been made more memorable if she hadn't disliked being handled by anyone, including me.

That's what I want you to avoid, and you can easily achieve that, and have a dog who is not only happy to be handled but positively enjoys it by following the 'handling plan' coming up next. This is the exact same 'handling' plan I give my puppy owning clients, so if you are self-isolating with a puppy, then this is something you should be doing regularly anyway.

I've included it in this book too, because I think it's a great way for fearful dog owners to use food to desensitise their dogs to being touched, which should make for less stress-ful visits to the vets and groomers, long after your self-isolation period has ended.

Teaching a dog who doesn't like being touched to enjoy it takes a lot of time and patience. Well, time is one thing you have on your hands right now, so make good use of it with these handling exercises, and you'll give your dog a near fear-free future to look forward too, and wouldn't that be nice?

Yes Dominic, it would!

Cool, let's begin.

Training handling skills

For this exercise you will need:

- your dog's collar and lead
- a bowl of kibble, with maybe some treats mixed in too
- a dog brush.

I like to do this exercise with my puppy or dog on a table, although you can do it sitting, kneeling or even lying down with your dog.

It's preferable to use a table because your dog is less likely (though not entirely less likely) to move off the table.

Also, and this is the big reason, getting your dog used to standing still and being handled on a table is the exact same setup he will face in the groomers and the vets.

Training your dog to be good at the vet's

Place a large cloth on the table and attach your puppy's lead to his collar. Lift your puppy on the table then hold the lead in one hand and keep it quite short.

Then place the treat bowl nearby and start grooming your dog.

I would recommend you teach your dog to tolerate being groomed with a brush even if he isn't a breed who needs any grooming.

At some point in your dog's life, you are going to have to inspect his hair for ticks, mites, chewing gum (yes, it happens) and to locate the piece of fox shit, he rolled in earlier in the day which is now making your dog smell like he crawled out of a coffin.

Well, all that is much easier to do *if* your dog will tolerate being handled and touched in all his nooks and crannies.

- Start with a soft brush or if that is too much for him just running your hand down your dogs back, then progress to going along the back and down one of his back legs.
- Next, you can stroke your dog from his head and then down his shoulder and down his front leg.

- As your dog gets used to being handled, you can progress to softly gripping your dog as you stroke him, kind of a light massage grip, not forgetting to talk to your dog all the time and tell him how clever he is.

Next, we move onto what your dog might feel is more invasive handling.

This is where the treats come in.

- Have your bowl of kibble nearby (not in front of your dog where he can see it, or he WILL eat it), and once again run your hand slowly down your dog's back, and down by his thigh, past his knee and down to his paw. Then pick the paw up and give it a nice gentle rub. Then pop his foot back down and say "Good boy" and give him a piece of food.
- Repeat this with <u>all four paws</u>.
- You should repeat the whole exercise with each paw, only this time when you hold the paw you are going to count to three before you place it down and reward your dog. Make sure you are smiling and praising your puppy all the time.
- Gradually increasing the handling time like this is going to gradually increase your puppy's tolerance for being handled.

That would be a good place to stop for a break. When I've finished any training or a handling session, I like to play a little game with my dog to reward him for being so good. He will eventually associate the game with the handling and training, and so playing helps your dog see the handling exercise as an enjoyable activity.

After a break, or even the next day, you can repeat this exercise, and in stages move onto your puppy's ears, eyes, mouth and bum.

Yep, you read that right. I said bum.

Don't worry; you aren't going fully internal, but it's good to get your puppy used to being touched and handled everywhere.

You never know what illness will require him to be handled by a vet. At some point your vet is going to check your dog's temperature with a thermometer up his bum, so get your dog used to this by touching around the bum area (obviously without actually putting anything up his bum).

Training your dog to enjoy having his ears touched

That sounds like an oxymoron. I mean, surely no one in their right mind would enjoy having their ears touched? I know I certainly don't.

However, I'm a human who can be reasoned with, and when I have an ear infection, I put my fears to one side, and I'm a big brave boy while the doctor checks my lugs (and if I'm really good I get a lollipop for my troubles).

Your dog, however, can't be reasoned with in the same way. You can't sit your dog down and say *"Look, fella, I know you don't approve of anyone raking around your ear, but you have a seed stuck in there which will get infected if we don't remove it, so be a good chap and sit still while we do the necessary"*.

Your dog will twist his head and make it impossible for the vet to do his job, unless … you spend a bit of time now getting him used to having his ears and eyes checked, so …

- Start by just massaging your dog's head and whole ear; then progress to holding the ear flap between your finger and thumb and gently massage, rewarding with kibble now and again. If your dog likes tummy rubs (and who doesn't?) then you can gently inspect your dog's ear with one hand while rubbing his tummy with the other.
- Then, if your dog is managing well enough, you can progress to the inside of the ear. Use a clean cloth and gently wipe the inside of the ear in a circular motion. Finger in, wipe, finger out, then a nice reward and cuddle. Well done, dog!

As you did before with the paws, you want to gradually increase the amount of time you can have your finger inside your dog's ear. Work up to 10 seconds, although this may take a few weeks to achieve by practising just a few minutes each day.

Easy eye checks

You can repeat the same routine with the eyes, as you did with the ears.

Start by holding your dog's head still for a second, as you look into his eyes. Gradually increase the time you hold him. Then you can get him used to having his eyes wiped by using a clean, damp paper towel or tissue.

All of my dogs have needed eye or ear drops sometime in their lives. Yours probably will too, and completing these short regular ear and eye check-ups now is going to make administering future medicines a cake-walk.

Manageable mouth examination

Finally, we have the mouth area. This is one place you will probably struggle to get immediate access to.

You can make it much more likely your dog will open his mouth by gently holding the top and bottom of his jaw with each of your hands, and then as soon as you have the mouth open simply pop a piece of chicken or another tasty treat in there.

This will at least get him used to readily opening his mouth.

Then you can start rubbing just your finger across your puppy's gums. As before, use the treats to reward him and gradually build up your puppy's tolerance for having his gums massaged.

Then you can add a small quantity of doggy toothpaste to your finger and make sure your puppy is comfortable before you move onto using a doggy toothbrush.

Doggy dentist

Doggy dental treatment can be expensive, so cleaning your dog's teeth once a month like this can potentially save you a fortune. Although the diet your dog is on also plays a big part in how his teeth turn out.

My Dogue de Bordeaux, Derek, is on a raw diet, and so because of the bones and lack of additives has pearly-white gnashers, while Sid has been on more dry food and consequently has more plaque on his teeth, which I have to remove using the method described above.

So that's the handling routine. Do this regularly, and your puppy will actually enjoy going to the vet's and being handled.

Handling health check

This kind of handling session also acts as a great health check for your dog. You will be able to keep a much better handle on his weight and any little injuries he picks up, *if* you regularly (weekly would work) do a handling session like this.

One of my previous clients owned a giant schnauzer who hated being groomed so much he actually had a heart attack. When she got the next dog, I made sure he was more than happy to be groomed. We had regular visits to the groomer's BEFORE he was even groomed just to meet them and get him used to standing on the table.

And I did a lot of work at home, using the handling techniques I have shown you, which I then built on by using scissors (clipped slightly away from the dog), electric razors and hairdryers (which I used to massage the dog with) to get him used to the feeling of being groomed and dried.

If your puppy is going to require regular grooming, then I suggest you follow a similar routine.

How to use food to make your dog love you

Finally, another thing you can do with food, just as you can with play and affection, is reward your dog for doing spontaneously good things.

In the trick training chapter to come I show you how to lure your dog into a sit, or a down, but you can also reward and encourage your dog to do what you want by 'capturing' his good behaviour.

So if your puppy decides to run towards you when you bend over to tie your shoelace, then reward him with praise, affection and even a treat. If you capture this behaviour often enough, then he will naturally start running towards you whenever you lower yourself onto your haunches.

Rewarding eye contact

Eye contact should also be rewarded regularly and with great enthusiasm by you. Personally, I want my dogs to think that looking at me is something worthwhile doing regularly, so I reward all eye contact with my dog. Not often with treats actually, but always with a smile and a stroke of the head, and a "Good boy".

Capturing behaviours like this makes it more likely your dog will look at you or 'check-in' with you when he is off lead at the park too.

Summary

- Food is fuel for your dog, and a good diet is essential for his physical development. Exactly how you use food will play a big part in how easy your dog is to manage. Using the food correctly means NOT wasting it by feeding from a bowl. Be sure to invest in lots of treat-dispensing toys to entertain your dog and feed him at the same time.
- Handling skills – Having a dog who is happy to go to the vet's and groomer's is a dream, and alternatively owning a dog who hates being touched, handled or groomed is a total nightmare; even simple jobs like checking his ears or removing thorns from his feet can

be fraught with danger. Make sure you do some grooming, handling and a general daily health check with your dog during your self-isolation period. You probably won't completely fix the problem, but you'll certainly desensitise him to make trips to the vets and groomers more bearable.

- Many a time I've been in the park and watched in horror as an owner repeatedly screams their dog's name in vain as he completely ignores them and continues arsing around. I feel like asking "Are you sure that's your dog's name?" but I don't. I'm nice like that. It does stress how important it is to teach your dog his name, and when you say it he should come to you because good things happen. Doing this consistently now will set you up to have a dog who recalls anywhere you let him off lead.

Chapter Four

Easy Peasy Trick Training for the Stuck at Home Pooch!

"Rambunctious, rumbustious, delinquent dogs become angelic when sitting."
Dr Ian Dunbar

One trick, you might be surprised, I don't recommend you teach your dog is a 'paw' or 'high five'.

There's nothing wrong with this trick per se; I just find once a dog has been taught to paw, it tends to become his default trick when he wants anything from you.

So if he needs the loo, he gives you his paw.

If he wants a treat or a drink, then he gives you a paw.

And if you don't act quick enough, he will start giving a paw more forcefully, which essentially means the dog ends up hitting the owner to get what he wants.

When he's a nine-week old puppy this isn't a problem, but fast forward a month or two and it's a different story. The problem is exacerbated when the dog is a large to giant breed, or if you have small children in the house who are more sensitive to being whacked on the leg by a puppy.

So no paw will be taught here, booooo …

But I do have seven magnificent tricks to share with you that are fun and purposeful. Yay!

First, let's clarify a few things.

Old dogs can learn new tricks. A trick is simply a behaviour performed by your dog to get a reward. The more tricks he can do, the more you can ask him to do to get rewarded from you.

Puppy's also, can and should do trick training. By teaching your puppy some tricks at an early age, you *aren't* trying to turn your new addition into some kind of puppy prodigy who will be competing on the next episode of *Britain's Got Talent* (although you never know *what* will happen *if* you catch the training bug …).

No, training your puppy with some cool tricks is simply a great way for you to start teaching him what is expected of him, and what he has to do to reach the venerable status all dogs aspire to, i.e. how to be a *'good boy'*!

Trick training will also help you learn about your dog's body language, and even more important for him, it will begin the process of teaching him about human body language.

And all the while you are training your dog, you are constantly reminding and reinforcing to him good things (toys, treats and affection) come from you.

This is how you make your dog fall back in love with (and want to be with) YOU.

Do you have a puppy prodigy or an old-timer?

It really doesn't matter! Your puppy is a sponge who is capable of learning new things very fast, and your older dog will soon learn how to learn new tricks to earn the rewards you have for him

Trick training is going to engage your dog's mind, and tire him out mentally, so he sleeps and settles more quickly. It will provide a vital alternative to outdoor running and playing during your self-isolation period.

Regular trick training sessions also help add structure to your dog's day and give you something to do with him instead of just cuddling …

Cuddles are awesome but any lazy moron can sit and cuddle a dog all day, and many lazy morons do just that.

It takes consistency and a commitment to training to have a really great dog, and teaching him to perform some tricks is going to be fun for you, your family *and* your dog; not to mention tricks are an awesome way to show off how clever your dog, and how much his behaviour has improved when guests are finally allowed back into your home, post self-isolation.

Where to start with trick training

We are going to start with the classic 'sit' and then a 'down'.

'Sit' is an incredibly useful trick that gives your dog something to do instead of jumping up at you, or anyone else.

Trick training

There are many ways to teach your dog tricks, but as usual, I'm going to show you the easiest way to do it, using a technique called luring.

Learning through luring

Luring is all about showing your dog what you want him to do. Think of it as using something like a ball or food to guide your dog into whatever position you want him in.

And I'm going to borrow the name of one of my first dog training clients (a fine female German pointer) called Aster to help you remember how to teach your dog anything using the luring method.

But first, we need to lose the 'e' from her name so we are left with ASTR, which stands for:

A – Attention
S – Show
T – Tell
R – Reward

Let's use teaching a 'sit' as an example, so I can explain how my ASTR method works.

You will need:

- a toy or treat
- your dog
- some enthusiasm.

'Sit'

First, make sure your dog has seen the toy or treat by putting it in front of his face (or nose for food). This is the first stage in the trick training process, you getting your dog's ATTENTION.

Slowly move your hand holding the treat from his nose to just above his head. Then wait for him to put his bum on the floor.

If he doesn't, just take it back to his nose again, and move it even more slowly above his head. Maybe change the angle this time, so you are going more above his head then back towards his neck (slowly) or above his head towards you.

Take your time with this and be patient.

Your dog doesn't know what you want him to do, but he will do very soon, and once he's got it, he will easily do it all.

This is you SHOWING your dog what you want him to do.

Once your dog has done it a few times, you can TELL him the command.

So once he starts sitting regularly, you should then say "Sit".

Your dog doesn't speak English, and it's much easier to pair the command to the action than it is to repeat ""Sit" 17 times while you wait for your dog to sit.

As soon as your dog's bum hits the floor, you say "Good boy" and give him his REWARD (a game of tug or a little piece of kibble).

Repeat this, and once your dog has done it four or five times and has the idea, *then* you can start to add the 'sit' command as his bum hits the floor.

That's your 'tell', so you tell him what you want. Repeat another four or five times until he is sitting as you say "Sit".

Phasing out the treats

Once your dog has the hang of it and is regularly following the command, try to lure him into position using just your hand.

Place the piece of kibble on a bench or in your pocket. Then when he sits, get the food out, make a huge fuss and give him a small piece of food.

You should repeat this until you think your dog is doing the action

when you say the command almost every time; then put the toys and treats to one side and have a little break.

In the break, you should put the kettle on and tell your dog how bloody clever you think he is, and give him some affection. I want you to go overboard with the affection and the praise.

Your dog will enjoy it, and he will associate the whole training session with having a good time with you. Using lots of praise and affection will mean you are not completely dependent on the toys and treats to keep your dog's focus on you. You will enjoy it too.

So there you go; that's how to teach a 'sit' using luring, and you have ASTR to help you remember which order to go in.

It's not hard at all, is it?

No, Dom, it isn't.

Don't forget you need to have your dog's attention before you start training a trick, so you should always play with him a little before you start. Think of this as a warm-up.

Training tips:

Be careful you don't use too high a value item of food when you begin your training indoors.

There are a couple of reasons for this.

Using a treat that is too tasty or a toy which is too stimulating is going to have your dog jumping at you to get at it. You want to use something he wants, but won't go mental for, so his regular dry kibble will do just fine for now.

The other reason is you will need to use the higher-value items when you come out of self-isolation, when you take the training outside more regularly, and there are more distractions around. Also, it just makes more sense to train this way.

If you were starting a new job, and on the first day at work you got a big fat bonus and a new car as soon as you walked in, then you would probably struggle to motivate yourself on days two, three and four.

So let's think long term and make your dog work a little even for a low-value treat.

Of course, you are going to use your voice and affection so that even the low-value food feels more rewarding for your dog.

So where do we go now?

Well, if you really want to progress with your training, you should do two things.

1) Start teaching another trick. I would recommend a 'down' then 'spin' followed by 'catch it' and then 'through the legs'. I have instructions for you to follow so you can teach each new trick using the same luring technique, just as you did with the 'sit'.

2) But just as important as starting something new is to lock down the trick you have just taught. So start practising your 'sit' in the kitchen and other rooms in the house, BEFORE you do the same thing in your garden or yard, and eventually the street and the park. Don't expect your dog to sit automatically straight away in another room on command, but each time you practise a trick your dog should pick it up a little quicker in each new room you practise in.

Make it easy for yourself and always have some food to hand. You probably won't need to do as much luring as you did in the sitting room, or if you do, you will more quickly be able to start luring with just your hand, but be prepared to use some toys or treats to get him going. One thing you absolutely must do is talk to your dog; say his name, and use praise and affection before, during and after whenever you practise anything. Then he will have fun and enjoy it, and he will want to do it again.

The second point is critical, as this whole trick section is the start of you building a new routine of things to do with your dog on a daily basis.

You will have a whole routine of activities which he loves doing with you, but we start this training indoors where it's easiest to learn. Then by the time your self-isolation is over, and you are ready to go for walks to the park, you will have already built an amazing bond with him, which will help you deal with distractions and keep him glued to your side.

Teaching other tricks:

'Down'

You can lure your dog to a 'down' from a 'sit' or a 'stand'. I will describe it from a 'sit' as that's the exercise we have just done but feel free to go from a 'stand' or whatever is easier for you.

So think ASTR, and first get your Kryptonite and get your dog's attention.

From a 'sit' position, move your hand from your dog's face area (to make sure he has seen the toy or smelt the food) and slowly move your hand down towards the floor in front of him.

You can encourage him to get it or follow it down to the floor. But don't say "Down" yet, remember. We are at the

'SHOW' part, where we show him what we want him to do.

You may have more success moving the toy slowly down between your dog's front paws, and he should slowly slide down into the 'down' position. Again, this isn't a race, so take your time with it.

Dogs are a bit like humans in that some are cleverer and quicker than others, and from experience, I can tell you my cocker spaniel, Sid, learned to do a 'sit', 'down', 'spin' and 'rollover' in the same time it took me to get some eye contact from Barry the Bordeaux.

Remember this isn't a competition, and you should challenge and push your dog, but go at a pace to suits him, and always make sure it's fun for him.

On that subject, with all these exercises and tricks, always reward your dog for trying, so if he even attempts a 'down' and slides down just a little, you should tell him he's a 'good boy'.

Encouragement is the key here. We want him to enjoy it and want to do it again, so make it pleasurable. You should never get to a point where you feel frustrated with your dog.

Be patient and if you think he's struggling with any of the tricks, then have time out, remind yourself it's not your dog's fault, that it's all part of a process, and have another go later on.

Training tip:

Some dogs just aren't keen on doing a 'down', so don't stress if your dog doesn't fancy it, or maybe try on a different floor surface.

If your dog keeps moving backwards, you could try the exercise with your dog's back end facing a wall or your couch. Then as you go from a 'sit' to a 'down', he can't back away from you. This sometimes helps them into a 'down' position.

Then as soon as your dog gets near a 'down' position, you can tell him he is a 'good boy' and give him some affection or a little piece of food. Repeat this, keeping it light and fun.

Start getting into a rhythm of practising something five or six times and then having a little break.

When your dog is going into a 'down' regularly, you can start to add the 'TELL' ('down') command as his chest hits the floor. Again, repeat five or six times.

There is a slightly quicker and more direct way to teach this to dogs that are particularly toy or food motivated.

Get down on your haunches with your dog, and make the toy or food 'come alive' to get his attention, and then move your hand from side to side across your dog's face, so your dog is following your hand intently and looks like he is watching a tennis match on TV. Then, quite quickly move your hand up just above your dog's head and then quickly down to the floor.

If your dog loves the toy or treat you have, he may well jump into a 'down' position, at which point you can reward him with a "Good boy" and his treat. As before, you should reward for just trying, so if he only goes halfway down, give him a reward a few times, and then gradually wait a little longer until he goes further down before you reward him.

'Stand'

Teaching your puppy to stand might sound a bit pointless. Surely you only ever want your dog to sit, right? Well, not so, mon ami.

You will need your dog to 'stand', and you will be glad you taught him this trick when you take him for a check-up at the vet's, or if he's a dog that will need regular grooming.

Teaching your dog to stand can be quite tricky, and it's even trickier if your dog doesn't do a reliable sit or a down yet, so make sure you teach *those* first.

One way to teach a dog to stand is simply to 'lure' him into a standing position when he is sitting or lying down in front of you. I would experiment a little doing it from both a sitting *and* a lying-down position, and then go with the one your dog more readily moves from.

If you can, start with your dog sitting or lying across the front of you. So you should lure him into a sit or down so his nose is pointing in the direction your right (or left if you are doing it the other way) shoulder is facing.

Then you take a treat and place it in front of his nose and then when he starts moving towards it to eat it, gradually move it away from him rising on the diagonal, so your dog has to 'stand' up to get the treat.

You can reward him for just attempting to stand, so if he moves his body only slightly towards the treat, then tell him he is a 'good boy' and treat him.

The next time you can wait until he moves his body slightly further into a stand position, then you gradually get him to stand and he enjoys the whole learning process.

Think back to when you were at school. You didn't just receive praise when you finished reading your first book. You were encouraged along the way.

First, you got a gold star for being able to read your ABCs. Then you started to put the letters together to spell words. C-A-T spells Cat (see how smart I am …). Then bigger words and sentences followed until finally, you could read a short story.

Your dog is going through a similar process with everything he learns.

So take your time, be lavish with praise, reward him for trying and enjoy the learning journey together.

'Touch'

One of the easiest ways to teach your dog to stand is to teach him to hand touch. This means he 'touches' the palm of your hand with his nose. In fact, this particular trick can be used to teach your dog all kinds of things from standing to heelwork.

Let's do the hand touch basics and then show you how to teach your dog to stand, using your hand as an example to get you started.

Teaching a 'hand touch' is also a good way to improve your timing when teaching tricks.

Ideally, you want to be verbally rewarding your dog with a 'good boy' as soon as he:

1. Plants his bum on the floor when doing a sit.
2. Places his chest on the floor when doing a down.
3. Or, in this case, as soon as his nose touches your hand.

The quicker you 'mark' the desired behaviour with some praise, the easier it will be for your dog to understand what you want him to do.

That's why this is such a good exercise to improve timing because as soon as you feel his wet nose touch your hand, you can say "Good boy".

Dogs are curious creatures, and yours probably won't need any encouragement to nose your hand when you present it to them, so let's try that first.

Start with your hands by your side or behind your back, and present one of your hands to your dog, holding it near his face.

He should move his head towards it and touch it with his nose. If he does then tell him, he's a 'good boy' and give him a treat. If he doesn't then repeat five or six times and try moving your hand slightly closer to him.

If he still doesn't seem interested in touching you then try rubbing some kibble on your hands. Your dog will usually smell the food and move towards it to investigate.

Then once he has got the idea, try doing it with the other hand. Then try presenting your hand ever so slightly further away from your dog, and he should reach towards it.

Once he is reliably touching both hands (which may take a day or two for him to master), then you can start adding the 'tell' or command, which in this case would be 'touch'.

Then you can start practising this all over the house, and outdoors in the garden too.

So hopefully you can see how you can use a touch to help you teach your dog to stand, but don't worry if you can't because I'm going to tell you anyway.

Obviously, you should ensure your dog is regularly touching your hand when you say "Touch" before you move onto this exercise.

So instead of luring your dog into the standing position using a treat as we did in the last exercise, this time you would simply present your hand slightly above your dog's head and wait for your dog to move into a 'stand' position as he touches your hand.

Touch is also a great way to get your dog (and especially puppies) used to the idea that human hands are friendly and nothing to fear, and it's also a great trick to help build your confidence if your dog is a little shy.

'Spin'

I love 'spin', and I get my dogs to do it all the time when we are out and about. This trick looks great and dogs seem to love it too. Again think

ASTR.

Attention – Show your dog the toy or treat. This trick is easier if your dog is standing up, and if he is a dog who likes to move away from you, then you should use a training lead to prevent him doing so.

Show – Show your dog what you want him to do. Hold the reward in front of his face. Imagine your dog is wearing a large top hat and slowly trace a circle around the outer brim of the hat. Your dog should follow your hand and circle round and return to something like the start position.

Tell – Say "Spin" once he has the idea, and you can lure him fully round quite easily.

Reward – This exercise usually takes a little while, and you should definitely be rewarding your dog for doing a quarter turn and then a half and eventually a full turn.

Take your time with this. A full 'spin' may take a few days or even a week to perfect, but there's no rush to get it done quickly.

Once your dog is following the treat and spinning more easily, you should just use the hand movement to trace the circle, and then reward the dog afterwards. Then in time, you can fade out the hand movement – you still say "Spin", but the hand movement is less defined. But this can take many weeks.

Don't blame the dog if he doesn't do it straight away, and give him lots of praise when he starts to turn round. This will make him feel good.

Once you have locked down the 'spin', why not teach him a 'twist'? That's just spinning the opposite way round. So start the whole exercise again, and be prepared for it to take just as long as the 'spin' did.

Training tip:

It's much easier to teach a 'spin' from a standing position. However, if your dog keeps sitting down (which he might well do if that's what you have just taught him), move backwards slightly and tempt him towards you with the treat, then as he stands up and moves, you can start to trace the circle around his head. He will already be moving forward by then, and it's easier to get him to continue the movement but go around than it is to get him to start a 'spin' from a sitting position.

'Rollover'

Puppies are floppy little critters, and it's great fun seeing them do a rollover without even realising what just happened. It's also super easy to teach them to roll over, but you really do have to be patient and take your time when teaching your puppy a rollover, especially the first part of the exercise.

Dogs of any age who are fit and able should be able to do a 'Rollover', and you'll have a lot of fun seeing which way your dog prefers to roll.

As you would imagine, you need to start this trick from a down position, and if you didn't imagine that then do so now, and make sure you wait until your dog is reliably doing a down BEFORE you move onto a rollover.

So with your dog lying in a down position in front of you, take a piece of kibble in your right hand, and hold it just in front of his nose, so he stays in the down position.

I'm assuming now you are on your knees with your dog lying down in front of you, facing you. You are going to use your right hand to get your puppy to roll over. Eventually, he is going to roll onto his right shoulder, and roll from right to left in front of you, as you are looking at him.

Start by slowly moving the treat from his nose down the side of his mouth and under his right ear. Your dog should follow your hand and start turning his head as if he is looking behind his ear. Then slowly move your hand with the treat in behind your dog's ear and over the back/top of his head. You really do need to do this quite slowly. The idea is for your dog to look behind as he follows the treat, and then as he follows the treat he flops over onto his side, and then he rolls over as he follows your hand as it moves over what would have been the back of his neck, but is now the front of his face, because he's rolled onto his back.

Some dogs get this trick straight away, but for others, it can take a bit longer, so don't worry if he doesn't get it as quick as he did the others.

Troubleshooting trick tip

If you move your hand around the back of his head too quickly, he will probably start turning his head to the left and following you, but then snap his head round the other way to grab the treat as it comes over his head.

It's a good idea to break this trick down into four sections.

Part one is to get your dog to simply look left as your hand moves down the side of his face. Do 'just' this part five or six times rewarding with a tiny piece of kibble each time.

Then in **part two,** you can start to reward your dog with a "Good boy" as he flops onto his shoulder. Repeat this four or five times, then have a short break and tell him how clever he is.

For **part three** you can offer the praise and reward as your dog rolls full onto his back (with his paws in the air).

And finally, in **part four**, you can reward your dog as he fully rolls over onto the other side. Drop the treat on the floor in front of him and give him a big old cuddle.

Then once your dog is doing a full rollover, you can start to add the command 'over' as you lure him over.

That's a rollover done. Hurrah!

'Through the legs'

This is another really easy trick, and I like it because it is a fun way to encourage your dog to come back to you.

You can use a toy or a treat, which you should first show your dog to get his attention. Then take a step back if you need to get your dog moving forwards and following the reward, and lure him towards you.

Place your legs fairly wide apart, but so you are comfortable, no full or half splits please … Then drop the toy or treat just between your legs and reward your dog with lots of praise when he picks it up.

Repeat this a few times, gradually dropping the toy further behind your legs so your dog has to gradually move further underneath you to get it. Then when he is moving through, you can say "Under" or "In there" or whatever you want your TELL command to be.

Training tip:

Always put your hand straight between your legs as you drop the toy or food, and don't go around the side of your body and drop it behind, or your dog will just follow your hand around your body.

Also, don't throw the toy or treat too far between your legs and behind you either. Your dog will probably just run around you to get the toy.

After a few days' practising, you should be able to direct your dog between your legs using the command and the action of pretending you are throwing the toy between your legs. Then once your dog runs through, he will look for the toy on the floor, which you will then throw to him and give him lots of praise and affection.

So that's my super seven tricks to start you off. I have picked these because they are fairly easy to teach, and I do them myself every day with my own and my clients' dogs.

All of these tricks require your dog to be fairly close to you, so when you practise them you are giving your dog a reason to be near you wherever you are, this makes the tricks perfect ones to teach in your home during self-isolation and they will help you to maintain good off lead control of your dog to keep him near you if there are social distancing restrictions to abide by.

We will go into your dog's nose a little later (not literally), but outside there is more air movement and, especially if you live in the UK, more moisture. Scent is essentially moisture, and your dog's nose is going to pick up many more scents than yours. These smells will be interesting to him, and he will want to explore them. This is why you need to spend a lot of time playing indoors and building up a drive that counteracts his desire to want to go and explore every smell that isn't you and your toy.

Tricks have real practical applications too. A great 'trick' you can use to help your dog learn how to behave around new people is to get them to demonstrate a trick with your puppy.

Let's be honest, sometimes family members and friends can be a real pain in the ass when they visit as they can 'undo' a lot of the good training you are putting in place. That is unless you put some rules in place for the family members too…

A great thing to do is to make everyone pass a 'training test' before they can fuss and cuddle your dog.

This is great for puppies and more excitable older dogs too.

Place your puppy is in the crate, or your dog in another room while you let the visitor in and explain to them that your dog gets a little excited when he meets new people so you need them to make him do a sit and a down before they can say hello to him.

Then give them a treat, let your dog out (if your dog is very excitable and difficult to control around people then it's a good idea to put them on lead until your dog settles down. Then show the guest how to do the trick. Then it's their turn.

Make sure they do a sit first and then a down; then they can pat the dog on the head and tell him he's a 'good boy'.

This routine might sound a little draconian, but it really works because it imposes a bit of structure at a time when your dog is going to be mega excited to meet someone.

It also teaches him to meet and greet people sitting or lying on the floor, and if he's sitting and lying on the floor, then he isn't jumping up!

One of my clients did this when their extended family of eight people turned up. He had them stand in a circle, and one by one each made Charlie the giant schnauzer puppy do a sit and a down. He behaved perfectly afterwards.

This is a great self-esteem boost for the visitor too because they are helping with the training.

If you still feel odd, just blame me and say this is what 'Dom the Dog Trainer' said you had to do, so you are doing it.

Summary

- Use ASTR to help you whenever you teach your dog a trick or anything new. If he looks at you blankly, he is not being awkward; he either doesn't know what you want him to do, the reward you are using isn't rewarding enough, or it's too complicated for him. Either way 'it's not the dog's fault', so take it back a few steps or break down the exercise and make it easier for him.

- Don't make the mistake of thinking tricks are just something dog trainers do. These tricks will give your dog a new lease of life, and they a great brain-game that teach your dog to focus on you. Teaching him some tricks will make it easier for you to distract him from the thing you don't want him to do. Tricks are great fun, and you will surprise yourself by how clever you and your dog really are once you start practising them.

Chapter Five

Your Dog's Sniffing Superpower

"The sense of smell in all dogs is their primary doorway to the world around them."

– Robert Crais

My youngest son, Toby, loves superheroes. And I mean LOVES them. His favourite is the X-Men. To explain quickly, in case you haven't seen them… the X-Men are a team of mutant superheroes who each have a unique power and a super-cool name to boot, such as Storm, Cyclops, Wolverine, and Iceman, and they are led by Professor Charles Xavier.

In the movie *X-Men: First Class*, we go back in time to when Charles first met and banded together the X-Men, who were then just teenagers. They all have their powers, but they are young and inexperienced, and they don't know how to control them. And because of this, their powers end up getting them into trouble. Professor X takes them under his wing and teaches them how to control their abilities, so they can live normal(ish) lives in society with other non-mutants (like me and you).

You shouldn't need me to tell you that your dog has some superpowers too. There are lightning-fast Greyhounds that can race around a track at speeds of up to 40 mph; tenacious terriers that will dig into a rabbit hole until you pull them out; scary-strong Staffies who can crush supposedly indestructible toys into tiny pieces; super swimmers like the Newfoundland that can glide through the water aided by their webbed feet, and crazy-intelligent Collies that seemingly work like remote-controlled dogs and can move a flock of sheep from one field to another.

But there is one superpower that all dogs share, and that is the gift of smell. Dogs possess the same five senses as us: taste, touch, smell, hearing, and sight. But, it is estimated that 30% of a dog's brain is dedicated to analysing odour, which is 40 times larger than the area that our human brains dedicate to the same task. We know for a fact that a dog's nose contains around 300 million olfactory receptors compared to our measly six million.

I love this example from Alexandra Horowitz in her book *Inside of a Dog*:

"We might notice if our coffee's been sweetened with a teaspoon of sugar; a dog can detect a teaspoon of sugar diluted in a million gallons of water: two Olympic-sized pools full."

There are dogs that can find a tiny piece of cannabis hidden inside a suitcase placed among 1000 other suitcases, and there are even dogs that are being trained to detect cancer in human beings. Medical detection dogs help alert people with diabetes when their blood sugar levels become low, which is a daily hazard for those with severe diabetes.

Now that kind of ability is not to be sniffed at…

This makes our dogs' noses around 1000 to 10,000 times better than ours, which pretty much makes your mutt an X-Dog. And a superpower like that needs careful control, otherwise your dog's nose will get him into all kinds of trouble, much like the children with superpowers in *X-Men: First Class*.

I'm sure you will be able to think of a few occasions where your dog's nose has landed him in some trouble in the past. Maybe he stole a chicken fresh out of the oven that was cooling on the top, or in the park, he found a not quite empty but discarded pizza box and helped himself to what was left. He might, for example, be retrieving a ball one day when he suddenly drops it, stands stock-still and then whips his head to the left, and you both think 'Squirrel!'

We know that with all great superpowers come great responsibility – the only difference with Spider-Man is it's your dog that has the superpower and you who has the responsibility for controlling it.

Playing some nose games with your dog will teach him that he can use his powers and have fun with you. To paraphrase John Rogerson, we can say control the toy, control the game, control the nose, and control the dog!

Nose games can easily be played at home as well as outdoors. This makes nose-work an excellent self-isolation activity.

In many ways, with the reduced exercise you will likely be doing during your self-isolation period, giving your dog an outlet for his sniffing ability is more important than any other activity.

Think how a bird, born to glide and soar through the sky must feel when he has his wings 'clipped' and is placed in a cage.

Well, in a similar way your dog has the ability to see the world through his nose, so to be denied the opportunity to sniff, explore and follow scent trails outdoors for an extended period of time, could be detrimental to your dog's mental health. To counteract that,we are going to give your dogs olfactory system a daily workout that will leave your dog fulfilled, and you feeling like a fantastic owner.

Teaching a 'find it'

'Find it' is a brilliant game and one I play with my dogs every single day, every walk even, and indoors is a great place to start.

Don't worry if you think your dog can't find anything; just think of it as a slower and more civilised version of a retrieve, and you will understand how easy it is.

The main thing to remember is you need to have something that your dog really wants to find, so if you're in the garden or further afield, I would use a number one or two item from your dog's toys or food Kryptonite.

Show your dog the toy and make sure he is interested enough in it to actually want it.

Keep the dog on lead to stop him from getting the toy straight away, and then you can place the toy somewhere really easy for him to find: behind a chair or cushion if you are in the house or behind a bush, bin or bench if you are in your garden.

It doesn't matter if your dog sees where you put the toy at first, as he will still be using his nose. We want him to find it, remember? You need to make the finding of the toy very rewarding so he wants to do it again.

Then just encourage your dog to go and 'find it' and give him lots of praise and affection when he does.

Repeat this four or five times until your dog has the idea. Then you can throw the toy behind a different thing, lead your dog a short way away from the area and then encourage him to go and find it again.

A huge mistake that almost all dog owners, including me, make with this game is that they rush ahead and try and make it too difficult by hiding the toy too far away.

Then when the dog struggles to find the toy, the owner thinks he either doesn't like the game or isn't very good at it, neither of which is usually true. You are the teacher here; how fun and easy you make the finding of the toy or food will very much affect how enjoyable your dog finds the game, how quickly he learns to do it, and how much he wants to play in the future.

Find the food

You can play 'find it' using food as per the instructions above, and there are many other games you can play in the house that your dog will love playing, and you will enjoy watching him too.

You can use a baking tray or some plastic beakers to hide food under. Place five or so on the floor with a treat or some kibble under three of them, let your dog into the room, and encourage him to 'find the treats'. This is an incredibly simple game, but dogs love it, and you are encouraging your dog to use his nose.

You can start by placing a bit of food on the floor in your house. Let your dog see you do it, and then encourage him to get or 'find it'.

Repeat three or four times, and then place the food behind a door or cushion, and tell your dog to 'Find it', which he will quite easily. Once your dog has the idea, you can gradually make the game more difficult. You could play the game with food already in a KONG and hide the KONG. Then your dog has to find it and work to get the food out. This is double the challenge, double the stimulation, and double the fun.

You can take this even further by placing something tasty in a KONG, then wrapping the KONG in some paper, and placing it in a small cardboard box. Your dog then has to find the box, rip the parcel open, and remove the paper to get to the KONG and the food. My Barry loves playing this game and seems to enjoy ripping up the box as much as he does finding the chicken.

Putting self-isolation to one side, these games are great to do if your dog is injured and on cage rest, and you can't exercise him as much but still want to give him some exercise and stimulation.

Some pitfalls with this game are that you need always to be present when your dog is ripping up the paper, as you don't want him ingesting any. Also, once he really gets into it, your dog won't necessarily differentiate between a box you have made and a parcel that's been put through the letterbox, as I have found out to my cost once or twice…

When your dog gets good at this, then move the game out into the garden or yard and use upturned plastic plant pots to hide treats or toys under.

Using Scent Games to help with Social Distancing

Just as we did with a toy, you can play the 'find the food' game in the park too. I play this game with toys and treats on a daily basis with my dogs.

Again, use a lead on your dog for control then either get him to do a 'stay' or hold the lead while you place some small bits of food over a park bench and watch your dog use his laser-guided nose to help him find the treats.

If it's safe to do so, then you can play 'sprinkles', which is just you throwing a handful of your dog's food into the grass and letting him go and find it.

Searching

Searching in this instance involves your dog trying to find you or a friend or family member. It's a great game to play when there are two or more people in your house (outside is more fun but start indoors).

As usual, I would start by one person playing with my dog with a toy or some food. This will help rev him and increase his drive for the toys and the games he likes playing with you.

Start with one of you holding your dog's collar or on a lead attached to his harness. (You can do this with a collar, but I think it's more comfortable for the dog to wear a harness.) The other person then plays with the dog with the toy and slowly walks away showing the dog the toy. (The dog at this point should be between the handler and hider.)

The handler stands still so the dog can't move forward.

The hider then continues to move backwards out of the room and hides in an another room on the same floor. Then as soon as the hider goes out of sight, you (the handler) encourage your dog to 'Find mammy' or 'Find Geoff' or whoever it is you are playing with. You hold the lead and just follow your dog. Take your time, as there is no rush.

Training tip:

If your dog is struggling to find the person, then they are probably hiding too far away, or they haven't played enough with your dog to get him interested in the toy they have. Remember we want to make it very easy for the dog to find them and get his toy; that way, he will enjoy the game and want to play again.

Repeat four or five times. If the dog is doing very well, the hider can get more creative with a hiding place.

Then on the fifth go, change the game a little and bring your dog's superpower into play.

This time, the hider shows the dog the toy or food as usual, but as they go behind the tree, the handler places his hand over the dog's eyes. Then when the dog is unable to see, the hider moves to a different but nearby tree (note the tree must only be a couple of metres away; we WANT the dog to find the hider!).

Then when the hider is in position, the handler continues the game as before. The dog will head off as before to where he thinks the hider is, and when he gets there, he will be very surprised to find no one there.

Here is the magical part, and this is the bit where you just need to shut up and let the dog work it out. If you are very observant, you will actually see the very moment his nose kicks in and the senses switch from eyes to nose: 'Now, where is my mum?' It's important you keep schtum here, and at the very most, just encourage him with a 'Where's your mammy gone?'

At this point, your dog's nose will take over, and he will slowly but surely start sniffing the air or ground. His nose will eventually pick up the scent, and it will lead him to the hiding place, at which point everyone should go mental and tell him what a clever little doggy he is!

You can repeat this game a few times, swapping handler and hider, gradually increasing the distance, and swapping the trees you use.

Just remember to keep it nice and easy and FUN for your dog, and if he can't find the hider, you have made the game too hard for him.

Training tip:

When outdoors be careful on hot days, because any kind of nose work can be very tiring for a dog. It will also be more difficult for your dog if it's warmer, as there will be less 'scent' on the ground.

Chapter summary

- Your dog's nose is his most powerful weapon, so please use it and involve yourself in how he uses it. Anything you can do to provide an outlet for your dog's sniffing ability is going to stimulate and tire him out too. You are going to love unleashing the superpower that is your dog's nose.

- When appropriate, try and use park benches, monuments, trees, and bushes as hiding places for the toys and treats your dog finds. If you do this regularly enough, your dog will start to look forward to it. He will look to you more when you reach each stop-off point on a walk, in anticipation of his next game of 'find it'. I also think using the location like this teaches your dog that trees and benches aren't just there to wee on, but they are an apparatus for us to use in our games, which again gives you more control of your dog.
- Birds have to fly, bees like to buzz, and dogs have to sniff things. The more you introduce nose games into your dog's daily routine, the greater a superhero you will become to him. I guarantee you will surprise yourself how much you enjoy playing these scent games, and your dog will relish the tests too. Whether it is food, a toy, or a loved one that he is searching for, it doesn't matter; just make sure your dog finds it rewarding and enjoyable. Using exercises and games that harness the power of your dog's nose is one of the most powerful and effective ways to influence him.

Chapter Six

Multi-dog Households

Training and Exercising More Than One Dog

So do these training methods, and games still work if you own more than one dog?

Yes, dear reader, rest assured they work if you have three, four, or even more dogs. I have two dogs, many of my clients own two dogs, AND we exercise the dogs daily in groups of up to 10 dogs.

However, there is a slight caveat to that.

If you really want to improve the relationship you have with each of your dogs, then you will have to spend more time alone with each dog individually than you do now.

Remember your dog is going to be most influenced by whoever or whatever he spends the most time with and consequently gets the most fun, stimulation, and excitement from. And if you have two or more dogs, then their main stimulation is probably going to come from each other.

So unless you have lots of time to devote to playing and training, then your dogs are going to spend more time with each other than they are with you.

There are two ways to look at this, of course. One is that the dogs will bond really well because they play, eat, and sleep together and the other is that as they bond so well because they play, eat, and sleep together, you, the owner, become less relevant to them. Let me explain that in a bit more detail.

We have already discussed how the easiest way to have a dog that listens to you is to be the most interesting thing in his life.

So the ideal is to be the one person that your dog looks to for all his affection, fun, entertainment, food, and exercise. If you do this, then you will have an amazing bond together.

Well, you don't need to be a dog psychologist to see that this becomes much harder to achieve when you throw another dog into the mix.

One dog at a time

I own two dogs, and I can tell you from experience that it's twice as hard (and more) to train two dogs than just one. I'm not down on people owning two or more dogs, but it's a fact that the more dogs you add to your family, the less time you will be able to spend with each individual dog. The likelihood that some of your dogs will develop behaviour problems may then increase.

There are a couple of ways this usually happens. The most common is that someone owns a dog that is generally pretty well behaved and they decide at some point that they would like another dog. The second 'new' dog receives some basic training, but because of work and general life commitments, he ends up spending the majority of his time with the first dog.

The first dog is usually fine with this, hopefully he is anyway, and the first dog will be older and usually the calmer of the two. The second or new dog spends so much time with the first dog that he sees being with another dog as the norm, in just the same way as the first dog was happy to be on his own.

In cases where the dogs do everything together, the second dog will end up seeing the first dog as his keeper and not you, the owner. In time he may become very dependent on being with another dog.

The first dog may be man's (or the owner's) best friend, but the second dog becomes a dog's best friend. The age and temperament of the first/older dog will have a big influence on how the younger dog turns out. If you already have a dog-reactive dog that is difficult to control, then unless you do a lot of training, it's highly likely you will end up with two out-of-control dogs that are difficult to manage.

Another example would be the owner who decides to take two puppies from a litter instead of just one. I know what you are thinking. What would be cuter and more exciting than getting a puppy, eh? What about getting two! Sadly, two sibling puppies rarely work out trouble-free. I have worked with clients who have done this, and the common theme every time is a lack of control over the dogs. That's not to say it's impossible to have two well-behaved dogs from the same litter, but getting two dogs like this sets it up from the outset to be much more difficult for you.

Think about it; the puppies come to you already incredibly well bonded as they have been together with their mother every day since they were born. By the time puppies are seven or eight weeks old, which is the time they would leave and join a new home, they have done all the dog-to-dog socialisation they need to do; they have learned how to play, and how to bite, all under the careful supervision of the mother.

Then a new stage of a puppy's life begins, and he learns how to bond and play with his new human family. During the crucial first four months, he is gradually and carefully exposed to things like cars, buses, carrier bags, fireworks, lollipop men, and everything else we want to get the puppy used to, so he grows into a confident, happy dog.

For a puppy that's raised on his own, other dogs will hopefully just be something that he treats the same way as he does birds he encounters on a walk or the bin lorry, i.e. something he sees on a regular basis but is nothing to get particularly excited about.

This is much harder to achieve when the main thing a puppy spends its time with is another puppy. We already know that dogs are playful; well, puppies are even more so. I can tell you from experience it can be hard enough to get one puppy to listen to you, so trust me; training two will be more than twice as hard.

Remember I'm coming at this from the sole objective of wanting to have an easy and happy life with my dog. So if you own more than one dog, then complete the dog audit for each dog you own and then prioritise spending time with each dog individually, giving more time to the dog that needs the most work. You will know which of your dogs doesn't listen to you as much, pulls on the lead more, or is more reactive to other dogs you meet, so prioritise and try and fix the biggest problem first.

There really is no silver bullet with this. I have helped many clients (both online and in-person) who owned two or more dogs, and the ones who were most successful spent more time with each of their dogs individually, building up a better bond and finding out what each dog liked, and then used that information to influence their dogs and better control them.

To me it makes way more sense to spend 10 minutes with each of my dogs individually, playing a game or practising a few tricks, than struggling to play with both my dogs at the same time and not really giving either the attention they want. I should also add that all of the owners reported that they really enjoyed this extra time they put into their dogs' training. Think of it as a daddy (or a mammy) date night that you get to enjoy with each of your dogs whenever you like.

So if you have more than one dog, then you know what to do, and if you have one dog and are thinking of getting another, remember that you can provide all of the fun, stimulation, and excitement your dog will ever need, and he doesn't need another dog in his life to be happy.

A period of self-isolation is a great opportunity to build a better relationship with both, or all of your dogs.

This isn't too difficult to do. Spending some quality time with each dog and start with a 'dog audit'. Find out what each of your dogs really like to play with, eat and where they liked to be touched and stroked. Then progress to playing with each dog using the games I've described so far.

Just five minutes a day of 'solo' time will have a huge impact on the relationship you have with each dog. If you are consistent with this over time, you'll notice a lot more focus on your from each dog, even when your other dogs are around.

Chapter summary

- The key to dog training is consistency. The more time you spend regularly training your dog to enjoy doing things with you, the easier he will be to control. This is also true if you own more than one dog. You can teach your pack to ignore other dogs and do exactly what you want, but you may find the easiest way to do this is with each dog individually first.
- This is exactly what I do when we introduce another dog to our group adventures. After an assessment, I will work, walk, and play with that dog on his own for a few weeks, until I have built up enough drive for a toy and taught him a few games to enjoy with it. I am basically teaching the dog that I am a really fun person to be with, so when he starts coming out with our pack, then his focus is more on me than the other dogs. It can be done.
- There will be people you know who own two dogs who will no doubt tell you how great it is to own two dogs. That their dogs get on fabulously well together and they would have 10 dogs if they could... Well, now you know a little better, so when you catch anyone saying that, just smile and nod and continue on your merry way with your one dog that thinks the sun shines out of your arse.

Chapter Seven

In Conclusion

This is not a book I dreamed I'd be writing. In truth, I wish I'd never needed to do it, but now that it's finished it feels more vital than any other book I've done.

I love nothing better than being outdoors with my dogs. I left my sales job and set up a dog adventure business in 2011 because I wanted to create a job where I could spend all day in the great outdoors with dogs.

It's true dogs love running, playing, exploring, swimming, digging, chasing, retrieving and all the other fun 'doggy' activities, and we enjoy providing that for them.

So, providing a training and exercise manual for a dog that potentially needs to stay at home for an extended period of time, feels very odd, even to me.

It's like putting together a manual to help a fish who's allergic to water, or a mole who doesn't like mud or a Tiger who wants to go vegan.

However, if there's one thing dogs have shown us since we first invited them into our hearth and home, is they are incredibly adaptable.

Over thousands of years, we have manipulated the breeding of dogs to produce helpers, hunters and herders that can round up a field of sheep, detect cancer treatments and win TV talent shows, so it shouldn't be beyond us to provide what is required to keep a 'house dog' happy.

The activities in this book are designed to help you supplement a reduced exercise regime with your dog, not replace one.

In times of crisis, we all need to adapt, and what we are doing in *The Dog Owners Self-Isolation Survival Guide* is simply providing what our dogs need to be happy and healthy, within the restrictions that self-isolation brings.

And your dog actually only needs five things to be healthy and happy.

Number 1: A suitable diet

It should go without saying, but all dogs need nourishing food and fresh water daily. Generally, two meals a day is considered to be better than just one big meal, and certainly, two smaller meals will be easier on your dog's digestive system. There are many ways you can and should use your dog's food to make his day more interesting and your life much easier, and we will go into this in more detail later.

Number 2 - Appropriate exercise

Wow, who would have thought it? Dogs need a certain amount of exercise and stimulation *every day*? This may seem a little tedious, but it's surprising how many people neglect their dog's exercise and then act surprised when behaviour problems develop very quickly.

How your dog gets his daily exercise is as important as the *amount* he gets, and if you can be the thing which provides all of your dog's exercise, stimulation, and entertainment, he will be much easier to control. You have the tools in your kitbag to do that now, even when in self-isolation.

Number 3 - Your dog needs to feel safe

More precisely, I mean a safe place to eat, relax, sleep, and exercise. This might sound pretty obvious, but your dog needs a non-threatening environment to live and exercise in, and you should aim to make your dog's life as stress-free as possible.

This doesn't mean he should have free rein to do whatever he wants. There aren't many more annoying things than a spoilt dog that lacks any kind of self-control, well, except maybe a spoilt child. The structure and routine you provide for your dog will contribute massively to how safe and content he feels.

So does your dog feel safe? Is he ever anxious either at home when he is eating or when you are out walking?

Dogs often won't do normal things when they feel threatened or stressed, and quite often the simple act of removing the stressful element and giving the dog something else to think about instead will do wonders for his well- being.

This is why you should look upon a period of self-isolation as an opportunity to give your dog (and you) a break from all of the distracting, disruptive and sometimes dangerous elements that can make walking your dog a misery.

Number 4 - Interaction

At the start of this chapter, I mentioned about dogs being rather unique creatures in the way they seem to thrive and even crave attention and play. Well, by play, I just mean interaction and having fun, and trust me, your dog wants some fun in his life. If you think that play is just something that your dog does with another dog, then you are about to have your eyes well and truly opened. Your dog doesn't really care where he gets his entertainment from, and most dogs will happily play with a human, a dog, a cat, or even a parrot, but who your dog is allowed to play with and sees as fun has a great impact on how he will behave.

There are loads of videos on YouTube showing dogs that have seemingly made friends with cats, birds, and even lions. If you search for Bubbles and Bella Best Friends, you will see a dog playing and interacting with an elephant. Bella even uses Bubbles as a diving board.

Sadly, a lot of our pet dogs get their main interaction and play from searching for and chasing birds or other dogs. Is it any wonder that trips to the park are so stressful?

Use this self-isolation period as an opportunity to reconnect with your dog and show him what a fun guy/gal you are!

Number 5 - Challenge

In her excellent book *Making Animals Happy,* Temple Grandin talks about an animal having four core blue-ribbon emotions, one of them being a 'SEEKING' mode. She points to research by Dr Jaap Panksepp, who describes the seeking mode as a combination of wanting something really good, looking forward to something really good, and curiosity. I think this pretty much nails how our dogs and all mammals live their daily lives.

So if your dog is looking for things to do, and I have no doubt that he is, then it's our job as the owner to provide the challenge and purpose that your dog is looking for. Use this survival guide as a reference book that will help you provide a series of daily challenges for your dog, which will make him happy and keep him out of mischief.

I call it providing your dog's daily challenges, mainly because I want you to think of this as something that you can provide for your dog. The challenges your dog faces each day will have a huge impact on how much control you have over him and how happy, content, and easy to manage he is.

So, whilst you might want to give your dog a lot more than just those five things (I certainly do too), you know that if every day of a self-isolation period we tick off those five basic activities, you are actually giving him everything he needs to feel like a dog.

I guarantee, if you do just half of what I suggest, then you will come out of self-isolation with a more attentive, focused and biddable dog.

And if you continue to play the games you played indoors at the park, then you'll have a 'sticky' dog that wants to hang around you, and not bugger off in search of fun.

To help you maintain great control of your dog at the park, and abide by social distancing restrictions, I've included a chapter of another of my books *Worry Free Walks How to transform your dangerous, difficult and devilish dog into a problem-free pooch that you're proud to take to the park* . You'll find the bonus chapter at the end of this book.

I have one more special resource to share with you in just a moment, but first I want to thank you for buying and reading this book. I truly hope it's made a small but positive difference to your life, and helped you better connect with your dog during your self-isolation period.

If the help has helped, then please send me an email and let me know what you found most useful.

You can contact me on dom@packleaderdogadventures.co.uk .

Also, please don't forget to leave a nice review on Amazon for me, reviews are the best way for this book to be found by other dog owners who also need help.

I wish you and your dog a happy, stress-free, well-connected future.

Stay safe
Love
Dom
X

Now, turn the page to get access to ***The Dog Owners Seven Day Self-Isolation Survival Guide Video Series.***

Your Special Free Gift

I hope this book was enjoyable to read, but most of all, I hope it inspires you to do more with your dog while you are confined in your home.

I appreciate there's only so much practical demonstration you can get from a book, so to help you move forward faster with your indoor training lessons, I am giving you access to **'The Dog Owners Self-Isolation Survival Guide Training Program'**.

This series of free dog training masterclasses will add lots of meat to the bones of this book. You will see me demonstrate with my own and my clients' dogs the simple training techniques I have described here.

This is a seven-day video program delivered daily via email.

Over seven days you will learn;

Day One – How to find your dog's kryptonite. The key to quickly building a bond with your dog is to find out their favourite toys, and treats, then using them to play games with the dog. In this first video, I do a live demonstration of a 'dog audit' with one of my own dogs. You can copy the step-by-step process.

Day Two - To build on the 'Finding the Kryptonite' from yesterday,on day two I'll send you my 'How to play with your dog' video. This will help you get your dog's attention and exercise him out indoors.

Day Three – To help you further master 'using the food' I've put together a Puppy Food Games Masterclass which will more clearly demonstrate a lot of the food games I talked about in chapter 2.

Day Four – To help you master the trick training in chapter 4, I will send you my Clicker-Free Trick Training Course. This is a short course that will show you how to quickly teach your dog five cool tricks.

Day Five – In this video, I'll show you how to turn your dog into a searching specialist. I'll show you how to teach your dog a 'find it', so you can play stimulating nose-games from the comfort of your front room.

Day Six – On day six, I'll show you how to teach your dog a 'leave it'. This is a great trick to promote self-control in your dog and will help you to get him to 'sit and stay' when guests arrive.

Day Seven - On day seven, you'll get 'The Derek Diaries'. Derek came to us as a naughty but loveable teenage tearaway, who was full of energy and mischief. We filmed all of the initial training and 'getting to know you' sessions I did with Derek, so you can see for yourself how I started to build a trusting relationship with him.

In 'The Derek Diaries' you will learn:

- Why we decided not to get a puppy and instead chose a rescue dog. I also walk you through the adoption process.
- How to stop a big dog from jumping up at guests, without shouting or turning away from him.
- How I got instant control of Derek on lead by ditching the harness and flexi lead.

- Why I didn't let Derek mix with my other dog until he settled in, and the big mistake I made on Derek's first night with us.

To grab the '**Dog Owners Self-Isolation Survival Guide Video** Series' NOW go to;

www.mydogssuperhero.com/survivalguide

About the Author

Dom Hodgson is a dog adventurer, 'superhero' dog trainer and the UK's most respected, sought-after and controversial pet business coach.

In 2011 Dom launched his first business, 'Pack Leader Dog Adventures', which revolutionised the dog walking industry by transforming the usual dog walking services from a 'boring toilet walk around the block' to a training adventure experience that helps busy dog owners with stay-at-home dogs enjoy a full, active and stress-free life.

In 2016 Dom wrote the Amazon-bestselling *How to Be Your Dog's Superhero*, which for the first time delivered a 'real-life' dog training blueprint that any pet dog owner can use to have more control and more fun with their dogs.

The Dog Owners Self-Isolation Survival Guide is really a one-off book, quickly written and produced to help dog owners all over the world to better manage their dogs during the Coronavirus outbreak.

Dom is known as the 'King of Canine Common Sense'. He is an in-demand speaker, and in his dog training seminars and pet business boot camps he delivers the same unvarnished, no-BS, jargon-free advice he dispenses in his unique writing style, which has won him thousands of dog and human admirers all over the world.

Occasionally, when invited, Dom will travel to speak at dog training clubs and to consult with dog trainers, walkers and groomers to help them grow their business. His seminar attendees describe the experience as hilarious AND life-changing, and his record in helping turn around failing pet businesses is unmatched in the industry.

To enquire about a speaking or pet business consultation email Beth at beth@packleaderdogadventures.co.uk

He lives in an old farmhouse in Sunderland in the North East of England with his wife and best friend, Beth, and two sons, Toby and Alex. Alex is also the Adventure Manager for Pack Leader Dog Adventures.

When not working, Dom can usually be found walking his dogs on the beach or sitting with his hens in the garden.

Turn the page to get your free, bonus chapter of *Worry Free Walks.*

Bonus Chapter from *Worry Free Walks : How to transform your dangerous, difficult and devilish dog into a problem-free pooch that you're proud to take to the park*

Available from Amazon and Audible

OPERATION 'DOG PARK'

"Why should we look to the past when preparing for the future? Because there is nowhere else to look"

- James Burke

You've done your preparation, and you know your dog's strengths and weaknesses. It's time to head into battle – and for that, you need a battle plan.

Okay, 'battle plan' is probably an exaggeration. What you really need is a plan of action that pulls together all of the tips and tricks you've learned so far and structures them into a simple, safe and stimulating 'dog park' routine that you both enjoy.

So your mission, should you choose to accept it, is to safely get to and from the park, while exercising and entertaining your dog in whatever time you have available. The walk needs to include activities that fulfil all your dog's daily needs, while at the same time eliminating any conflict and complications, so you both feel safe, and you, in particular, feel in control of the situation at all times.

So, maybe a battle plan is a good description after all!

The Walk Starts at the Front Door

Don't make the mistake of thinking the toys and treats weighing you down are only to be used once you get to the park. You can, and should, be using them to get eye contact from your dog on the way to the park too.

In fact, if you followed the advice from the previous chapter and you spent some time pre-exhausting your dog before you left the house, then that will give you some momentum, which you can build on as you walk to the park.

Your dog isn't the only one who needs to focus, and you will benefit hugely by just talking to your dog as you walk.

Tell him what a good boy he is and what fun games you are going to play at the park. If you need to then show him the toys and treats you have with you. This constant communication forms the bedrock of the relationship you have with your dog and will make controlling him at the park much easier.

Depending on how far you have to walk before you reach the park, you may want to stop and play a few games along the way.

Play Pitstops

It's a particularly good idea to do this if you have a dog that simply can't wait to get to the park. Playing some games, and practising some tricks en route will convince him that he has no need to rush, and that good things can happen on the journey too.

I regularly do this with my own dogs. We will find a small patch of grass, and after they have toileted, I will play a short game of tuggy or find it.

Arriving at the Park

I like to do a quick recce of the park as I approach it.

Is there a group of kids playing football, or are a family having an impromptu picnic? If so, you might be better heading to a quiet area in the park, or maybe try a different park altogether.

At the very least you can enter knowing you need to be wary of the things that could be a hazard for you and your dog.

How successful you are at getting your dog's attention at the park will, in part, depend on how much time and effort you spend playing with him at home. The owner who plays and interacts regularly will have next to no trouble getting their dog's focus at the park.

Dogs learn through trial and error and repetition.

If your dog tries something and he likes doing it, then he will be more likely to do it again.

Then the more times he practises that behaviour, the more ingrained it becomes in him until it becomes part of his routine and something he does automatically.

So if you play regularly with your dog at home and in your garden, and en route to the park, then pretty soon he will start to look at you more often. And when you take a tennis ball, tuggy toy or piece of food out of your pocket, he will know exactly what the game is you are going to play, and what he has to do to get the reward.

It's fairly simple stuff, but it's incredibly effective.

So, play these games often and vary the resources you use, make it FUN for the dog, and leave him wanting more (which he will do, *if* you have played enough).

Plan Your Walk (And Then Nail It!)

This is where you need to put a bit of thought into the walk.

Most dog owners just wander aimlessly through the park with little thought or attention given to their dog, unless the dog is doing something wrong.

They set off with no idea of what they are going to do and end up trying to deal (often unsuccessfully) with all the hazards as they crop up.

These hazards (birds, rabbits, other dogs) shouldn't be a surprise though because you see them every day, and with a bit of preparation and forethought, you can deal with most situations before they occur.

Remember, this is the highlight of your dog's day and his opportunity to blow off steam and enjoy himself. He will do that with or without you, so make sure he is enjoying himself with you, and not without you.

Walk With a Purpose

You need to plan and execute as best you can what you're going to do at each stage of your walk.

So before you set off, first you should warm up your dog and remind him that you have things that he likes.

Practise a few eye-contact exercises or a catch-up game. Chuck a ball a short way down your hallway while he is on lead and then take it from him and set off.

If your dog is a puller, is reactive or even just high energy, then it will be better for you to play a bit longer to really take the edge off his energy levels.

If this means a 20-minute walk is reduced to 15 because you spend five minutes playing before you leave, then so be it. The people who do this will have the most success.

I guarantee it.

Time to Light a Fire

I'm not suggesting you throw a match into a park bin; that would silly, not to mention dangerous. No, I'm talking about a metaphorical fire.

In a survival situation, a fire is essential. It provides heat, warmth, light and a sense of security.

And if you want to survive the dog park, then you need to provide the spark which becomes the fire that will be the centrepiece of your walk together, and you do this through play.

The first rule of fire making is to make sure you are in a safe place.

So, before you even think about letting your dog off lead, do a quick safety audit.

Assuming all is well you can move to the next phase.

You have no need for kindling and lighter fuel though; all it takes is some energy and enthusiasm on your part.

Much of what follows in this chapter comes straight from the procedures manual of my dog adventure business Pack Leader Dog Adventures.

Over the last five years, I have developed a signature system that enables us to maintain great control of the dogs in our care, all the time. You can apply the exact same system to enable you to enjoy super safe walks with your dog too. And if you are a dog walker, then you should check out the Professional Dog Walkers Academy by going to:

www.growyourpetbusinessfast.com/pdwa

Here are the bullet points:

- If you did your homework and followed the action points in the previous chapters then you should be fully aware of what toy and treats your dog likes playing with. And if you spent time regularly playing games with your dog, then you should by now have supercharged his favourite toy, so as soon as you take it out of your pocket your dog's face lights up, and his tail starts wagging.
- So while your dog is still on lead, show him the toy (or food), tease him a little and get him interested in it.
- Here we are building up his drive and shifting his focus from the environment to you.
- Then when your dog is showing a great deal of interest, you can ask him to do something to get the reward. A sit is the most common trick but don't be limited to that. You can do spins, down, jumps and a whole host of other tricks. The trick itself is not important. What you are doing here is testing your dog to see if he is paying attention to you.

- As with any test, if he passes, he should be rewarded, so make sure you give your dog constant feedback and tell him how well he is doing.
- By doing this, you get your dog focused on you and the toys, *and* you reinforce to him that you are the most interesting thing at the park.
- Once you have your dog moving around and following you, you need to move onto the next stage and get him 'recalling' towards you.

Many Happy Returns

Give your dog as much slack as your leash will allow and take a couple of steps backwards and call his name in a cheery happy voice. He should follow you and when he catches you up, you can tell him what a good boy he is, and reward him with his toy, or food.

Repeat this again, only this time jog a little further away before you reward him.

On our dog adventures, we like to repeat this recall test at least five times *before* we allow the dog off lead.

We do this with all the dogs who take part in our adventures. This simple exercise is one of the key factors behind me establishing my Pack Leader Dog Adventures as the UK's number one dog adventure company.

I'm telling you this not to brag, but rather to show you how we maintain great control of the dogs we look after.

If we can take eight dogs to a park (all of whom belong to our clients and not us) and through playing these simple games get their attention laser locked onto us in the middle of a busy park, then I'm sure you can do the same with your dog.

If the kryptonite is the spark, then the tricks and the recall game are the tinder and kindling that get the fire going. The oxygen (or wind) needed to make the first catch light comes from you and the energy and effort you put into the games.

Then once the fire is burning bright and your dog is fully focused on you, it's a matter of keeping the fire going throughout the walk. And we do that by periodically throwing logs (okay, enough with the fire analogies already!) or in our case 'playing games' with our dog at intervals around the park.

Circuit Training for Dogs

Circuit training for humans involves performing a series of exercises in a special order, called, unsurprisingly, a circuit.

Each activity takes place at a 'station' and when the instructor yells 'Time!' everyone moves to the next free station.

There are many health benefits to human circuit training, but the main one is you won't easily get bored.

You move quickly through 8–10 exercise stations to work different muscle groups, with little or no rest between stations.

You can take some of the elements of circuit training to help you devise a 'training routine' that takes you around the park and stops your dog becoming bored and losing focus.

So, your circuit may look something like this:

You arrive at the park and go through your full 'fire lighting' routine.

Then you can start your walk around the park. Keep talking to your dog and if you come across another dog on lead (or any other distraction) then use your kryptonite to get your dog's focus back on you.

1st Station: After a few minutes you arrive at station one. This might be near a park bench or tree. The location itself doesn't matter, but I would stop at a point where I had a good view of approaching dogs.

Now you can play one of your dog's favourite games. Two toys or a tuggy game will do, whatever your dog likes playing. You can have a long lead attached to your dog while you are playing this game. In fact, I would recommend you leave a lead on; it will put your mind at rest and allow you to concentrate on the game.

Then once you and your dog are worn out you can stick his lead back on and carry on circumnavigating the park.

2nd Station: Five to 10 minutes later you arrive at station two where you can play another game with your dog. This time you might use the food you've brought and practise some tricks (again on lead if you need to). If there's a park bench nearby, you could practise jumping over, and if you are feeling generous, you can let your dog have a go too. Seriously though, any kind of environmental stimulation like this is great fun. Just make sure it's safe for your dog to do the tricks.

Then you can head off on the walk again until you reach the next station.

3rd Station: This time, you might just want to sit with your dog and give him a little groom with a brush you've brought. Grooming like this, even just with your hand, is a great way to bond with your dog. It also acts as a daily health check too and is well worth doing.

If your dog doesn't like being groomed then use the food you've brought to distract him while you gently brush or stroke his back. Over time you can build up his tolerance to being touched, which will have the added benefit of making him easier to handle for a check-up at the vets.

Then you can continue with your walk until you reach the final station.

4th Station: At the end of the walk I like to play some scent games with my dog. So I will hide some treats or his toy around a tree stump or scatter them over a park bench and let him find them using his nose.

Nose games like this are a brilliant way for your dog to show off his superpower and it tires him out too. It's also a great way to get rid of the last of the treats you took with you.

So there you go. Four stations but it could just as easily be six or eight if you wanted to add more activities and games.

You could even just repeat the game you've already played. Trust me, your dog won't mind playing fetch, tuggy or find it again and again, until the cows come home, or until you both head home.

And you can mix and match the activities and games, depending on which route you take around the park, or indeed which park you are at.

The idea behind the circuit training is to encourage your dog to check in with you at regular intervals throughout the walk. By interacting with him often, playing games you know he enjoys, you will quickly transform him from a disinterested dog, into an attentive hound that is a pleasure to be with.

When to Rest?

I know what you are thinking now, this circuit training lark is all well and good, but when do I get to enjoy the walk? When is the downtime for me and my dog?

Well, you can have a 'time out' whenever you like, and I highly recommend you do. You need some time to stop, look around and smell the daisies and so does your dog.

Any time at all during the walk you can allow your dog some chill time to do his ablutions and check his pee-mail (I love that joke…).

Just make sure you do a quick safety audit and if the park is busy, or if your dog has a history of running off into the distance, then stick a long lead on him before you do.

But don't switch off completely. In my experience, this 'doggy downtime' is usually when my dog forgets all of the training and remembers how interesting squirrels, pigeons and other dogs are.

So downtime, chill time, sniff time or whatever you want to call it is to be recommended, just make sure you move the dog from 'drive' gear into 'park' mode and you do that by using a 5 or 10 metre lead. This acts as a nice safety net and will allow him to do whatever he wants, and you to reflect on how awesome a dog owner you have become.

Action Point

Let's recap your new structured walk, but don't get stressed about the word 'structure'. A planned walk doesn't need to be boring and complicated.

A simple plan would be:

- Take stuff with you. Some toys, a handful of kibble and chopped up bits of leftover chicken will do.
- Practise lots of eye contact as you walk away from the house. Let your dog see, smell and maybe taste some of the chicken.
- I would carry his favourite toy in one hand, and lure him into the heel position as you walk. Keep talking to your dog. Praise him when he does something right and feed him kibble, and the occasional piece of chick-en when he is walking calmly by your side.
- At every kerb, I would practise a sit and maybe a down (and back to a sit again).
- Find a small patch of grass that is about halfway to the park and do a 'Play Pitstop'. Let your dog have a sniff and toilet, and then play a short game of tuggy or a catch-up game.
- As you approach the park, do a quick recce to make sure all is safe, and as soon as you enter, find a quiet area and start playing with your dog.
- Start with some on lead games and test his focus with a few tricks. With your dog still on lead play a catch-up game, which will act as a nice bridge between the off and on-leash exercise. Play several of these games if you need to.

- Start your 'canine circuit training' and progress around the park playing games and having fun at regular intervals. This will teach him to look to you for fun and make him want to be with you.
- Save a super tasty treat for the end of the park session and give it to your dog when you stick him back on lead.
- This might seem like a lot of work, but all it really does is provide a routine that minimises the opportunities for your dog to get into trouble, and it gives you the tools and a plan of action that will enable you to take control and start enjoying exercising your dog once more.

Worry Free Walks : *How to transform your dangerous, difficult and devilish dog into a problem-free pooch that you're proud to take to the park* is available from Amazon or Audible.

Other Books by the Author

All available from Amazon and Audible

Dog Training Books

How To Be Your Dog's Superhero: Transform your dastardly dog using the power of play.

Other Books in the Street-Smart Dog Training Series (1–3)

Worry Free Walks – How to transform your difficult, dangerous and devilish dog into a problem-free pooch you are proud to take to the park.

The Perfect Puppy Project– The ultimate no-mess, zero-stress, step-by-step guide to raising the perfect puppy.

The Hungry Games – Discover how you can bin the bowl and use food to play, train and entertain your perfect pet dog.

Pet Business Books

Walk Yourself Wealthy: The quick, easy and no-BS guide to transform your passion for pooches into an insanely profitable and fun dog-walking empire .

The Ultimate Pet Business Plan: How to launch, grow and scale an outrageously profitable, impactful and fun pet business that dominates your local town.

Printed in Poland
by Amazon Fulfillment
Poland Sp. z o.o., Wrocław

57452944R00074